Praise for *Breaking Through!*

Individuals and families struggling with addictive disorders should read **Seasons in Malibu's** inspirational stories of hope. These stories not only show the universality of addiction but also how an effective and strong treatment team can change lives.

> — Reef Karim, M.D., Addiction Psychiatrist and Television Host

In *Breaking Through! Stories of Hope and Recovery,* the authors create a dialogue that individuals and families can relate to in such a beautiful way. These stories about the human experience are quite touching. So many people suffer and feel so alone in their struggles. This book helps any reader understand that you can get out of the darkness. It explains what addiction is about, and that there is real hope and sustainable, long-term recovery. *Stories of Hope and Recovery* is written for anyone who has been touched by addiction and will help people relate, learn and find a way through to the light.

> — Erica Spiegelman, Interventionist and Author

With drug related deaths traumatizing the country, **Breaking Through** helps us realize two important facts: First, there is no bias. Addiction cuts across gender, race, class, ethnicity and geographic location. Second, **Seasons** demonstrates that with both a comprehensive and multidimensional treatment approach, hope and recovery is very possible!

    — Ashley Benjamin, M.D. Addiction Psychiatrist

Breaking Through! Stories of Hope and Recovery does a great job of inviting you into the client experience and what one can expect when in treatment. The reader can rest assured that somewhere in these pages their story exists.

    — Damon Raskin, M.D. Board Certified
      Addiction Specialist

Breaking Through!

Stories of Hope and Recovery

Dr. Mark Stahlhuth and Dr. Nancy Irwin

WORLD CLASS ADDICTION TREATMENT

SEASONS
IN
MALIBU

Breaking Through! Stories of Hope and Recovery
Dr. Mark Stahlhuth and Dr. Nancy Irwin

Published by Jackson Deere Press

978-0-9983802-0-9 (Paperback)
978-0-9983802-1-6 (eBook)

Library of Congress Control Number: 2016963700

This is a work of fiction. Names, characters, businesses,
places, events and incidents are either the products of the
author's imagination or used in a fictitious manner. Any resem-
blance to actual persons, living or dead, or actual events is
purely coincidental.

Contents

Contents

INTRODUCTION:
Seasons in Malibu
World Class Treatment

Break through moments in life. We all have them; moments leading to insight often come at critical times. At **Seasons in Malibu Addiction Treatment Center,** we know that sometimes a breaking through kind of moment can trigger a client's desire to stop the madness of addiction, madness that prevents one from living a quality life. Frequently, clients experience these moments when they enter treatment. When nurtured by the therapeutic process, these moments can lead to insights that spark change.

Breaking Through! Stories of Hope and Recovery is a collection of stories offering hope to those standing at the crossroads of addiction. We hope these stories inspire. We believe in hope at **Seasons in Malibu.** Coupled with lots of hard work, our clients can and do reclaim quality lives stolen by addiction but only when they are willing to work hard. At **Seasons** we also believe in the power of sharing, in our groups, in our family sessions and even when we gather in our dining room to enjoy delicious food prepared by our chefs. Sharing is always encouraged here, that message delivered daily to **Seasons'** clients we now share with the reader in ***Breaking Through! Stories of Hope and Recovery***.

Today, we know much more about addiction than we did back in the 1930s when Bill W. decided to "out" this malady plaguing our culture. Addiction is a killer of lives, families and dreams. Addiction kills hope. But it doesn't have to. Conquering this enemy requires commitment to living a sober life. By reading these stories, a compilation of profiles that do not identify any one person, instead focusing on behaviors common to those suffering from addictions, we hope families as well as those in addiction's grip feel less alone in the struggle to stop this madness.

There is comfort in knowing you are not alone. If you recognize yourself or someone you love in these stories, you will also learn how some of our clients wrestled with this formidable opponent called addiction. We do this by offering "snapshots" of hard work clients have done at every level: physical, mental, emotional, intellectual and spiritual. Hard work done daily for weeks, and sometimes months, to understand and develop skills needed to foster change in viewpoint, behavior and lifestyle.

Seasons in Malibu has no interest in sugar-coating reality. Not everyone beats addiction. We know it kills; news media outlets consistently report on sad stories where addiction won. Another reason to offer this collection. The **Seasons in Malibu** treatment team believe chances of beating this opponent improve significantly with the right team in place. That's why from day one, beginning at admission, we begin to plan for our clients' discharges. At **Seasons in Malibu,** we believe it does take a village to beat addiction. It's that formidable an enemy.

The stories offered in ***Breaking Through! Stories of Hope and Recovery*** include diagnosis, family history and overview of effective treatments. Breaking through-like moments nurtured during treatment that helped shift thinking and/or feelings is the focus of this collection.

At **Seasons in Malibu,** we believe treatment is not a "one size fits all." Sometimes, individual therapy sessions helped a client see a family issue in a new way and/or helped a client let down his/her guard so change could have a chance. Sometimes, a breaking through-like moment is sparked when a client hears something said in a SMART Recovery session. These moments also happen quietly. Days and/or weeks of participating in our therapeutic community, paddle boarding in the blue Pacific and/or relaxing by the pool after a therapeutic massage often spark these moments worthy of journaling, which we encourage all of our clients to do.

At **Seasons in Malibu,** we believe these moments lead to insight. Once understood and nurtured through the therapeutic process delivered by our highly qualified **Seasons** team, insights gained help our clients build sturdy bridges to long-term sobriety. That's where hope lives.

In *Breaking Through! Stories of Hope and Recovery* our wish is that those searching for their village find it in the stories presented in this collection.

> Don Varden
> Chief Executive Officer and Founder,
> **Seasons in Malibu**

For further information about **Seasons in Malibu World Class Addiction Treatment,** please visit us at www.seasonsmalibu.com or call one of our Caring Admissions Counselors at 866-780-8539.

THE LOST SON
Manhattan/Los Angeles:
Chronic Cocaine Addiction

David remembered waking up in the dark hotel room. He couldn't tell by the light if was late or early. He had no idea what day it was either. He couldn't find his cell phone. He dragged himself from the bed into the bathroom. What he saw in the mirror made him shake. His face was cut in several places. His right hand was swollen and from the stench in the room and on his person, he knew his bowels and bladder had released during the time he lay there. He was freezing. He stripped off his wet clothes and grabbed the hotel bathrobe.

No recall at all, from the time he landed at La Guardia to waking up in that room, David couldn't remember a thing. Nothing. A cart and several plates of untouched food were next to the bed on one side and on the other, a nightstand filled with drug remnants of several kinds. None of it coke. The food had been there a while. The bread was stale and the sauce on the chicken breast had congealed on the dish. The sight made him sick. He ran back to the bathroom and retched. For several more minutes that's all he could do.

Later, he admitted his first instinct was to use coke. Desperate to feel better, he resisted the urge to score. This time was different. He was in that hotel room because of a scheduled court date he had to attend. He'd flown in the day before the custody hearing date. The evidence of his own annihilation in that room told him the date had passed. His soon-to-be-ex-wife would have been the only person standing in that courtroom not shocked when he didn't show up.

He hadn't planned to use. He promised himself he wouldn't. Another late day on set and a very early flight to NYC were his excuses. One last time. He knew he needed to be clear headed in that hearing room so he promised himself he would not use. Except he did. His Ex was fighting for sole custody with supervised visitation. She knew he could not be trusted alone with their three small children. She was doing the right thing. This high level film and TV star America so loved had reached a new low. He took another look at himself in that mirror, examining the wounds on his face, the "leading man" face that had made him a star. He called his wife, barely able to speak. He begged her to find him a treatment center before he killed himself. Two days later, David admitted himself to **Seasons in Malibu** Treatment Center. His estranged wife accompanied him.

**Meet David:
Manhattan/LA
Cocaine Addiction**

David woke up in a New York City hotel from a three-day drug binge, triggered by his drug of choice, cocaine, along with tequila and several other drugs. This forty-seven-year-old highly successful film and television actor had been using cocaine recreationally since his college years. David described himself as "lazy" in his youth, dropping out of college mainly because he lacked energy to study. Since childhood, he had been plagued by a lethargy that confined him to his bedroom for days at a time, a reality he just accepted. No one was more shocked than he was when at age twenty-one, while walking down a Manhattan street in the fashion district, he was approached by an agent. Within one week, his extraordinary good looks had landed him his first modeling gig. Two months later, David was cast in a Broadway show that became a longstanding hit and established his career. During his quest to keep up with this fast track success, he discovered cocaine. He liked it not just because of the energy lift it offered; cocaine lifted his lethargy, too. David knew how much better he felt on cocaine and for that reason kept an eye on usage, always quitting before starting a new project. Once settled into the routine on set, he'd begin to use again but his restraint kept the drug manageable. However, once his dying aunt revealed the family secret two years prior to his **Seasons** admission—that she was his birth mother and his mother was really his aunt—his ability to restrain his cocaine use collapsed.

Seasons Admission

David was grateful his estranged wife was willing to help him. Though she made it clear her decision regarding the custody arrangement had not changed, she hoped for their children's sake that finally he would get some help.

As David talked of his mood swings, his wife confirmed his view. He was always prone to them. Initially, she assumed his moodiness was part of being an actor. However, once he found out about his birth mother, his mood swings became much more frequent and his desire for cocaine increased. She said the last two years were a living hell and she and the children had moved back to New York three months earlier. She recounted the incident that had triggered her exit and filing for divorce. David had been kicked off the set of a new movie he was filming for being intoxicated and belligerent. Unfortunately, this information was leaked online and it went public. His face covered every tabloid paper and his wife was harassed by paparazzi who followed her to their children's school. For several days after the tabloid stories appeared, David couldn't be found. One week later, he showed up at their home looking haggard and dirty. The kids had returned from school in time to witness an explosive confrontation that included David threatening his wife, hurling glassware and a neighbor calling the police. Though he had calmed down by the time the police arrived, David was handcuffed and arrested. His wife filed a restraining order and within one week, moved their family to New York.

Family History

David described his childhood as ideal. He came from upper-middle-class Westchester County, New York, the only child of a couple who doted on him. He went to all the best schools and in his first school production at age ten, David's mother knew her son had something special. She used to call it "star quality," recalled David. The memory made him smile, the only time he did during the **Seasons in Malibu** admission.

His life dramatically changed soon after his thirteenth birthday when his mom was diagnosed with breast cancer. She was gone by the time he turned fourteen. She never said a word about his birth mother, nor did his father. It was his aunt's dying that prompted her to tell him what his mom and dad had not. She was his birth mother. He was born when she had just turned sixteen. His birth father, a hotel employee in the city, left town soon after she told him. Too young to take on the responsibility, her older sister and husband, devastated that they couldn't conceive, offered to raise her baby as their own. The family decided to pass the baby off as her older sister's newborn.

David's family kept the secret well. When he learned this truth two years prior to entering **Seasons,** he became enraged at his dad and deceased mother. During this two-year period, David's career also soared to new heights. With two films and a hit TV series, hotel rooms and private planes became home to him. Meanwhile, in Los Angeles, his wife struggled to keep their young family together, knowing what few knew. Her husband's cocaine consumption was out of control.

Detox

For two years before admission, David's daily intake of cocaine had neared three to four grams/day. He used other drugs that included alcohol, Vicodin and Xanax, but cocaine was his drug of choice. Detox included a five-day medical withdrawal from all drugs.

Three weeks into treatment, **Seasons'** psychiatric medical team evaluated David's "blues" and recommended a trial of antidepressant medication be prescribed in order to assess/evaluate his response before discharge. David readily agreed.

Community Based Support Groups

Seasons in Malibu is known for its multi-dimensional approach to drug and alcohol addiction treatment. This includes all evidence-based modalities, including SMART Recovery and Alcoholics Anonymous ("AA"). **Seasons** doesn't mandate its clients attend these groups but is open to and embraces all community based self-help groups. In David's case, he felt comfortable in A.A.

David was tremulous for the first several days after admission but only once did it keep him from attending meetings. He embraced A.A. meetings almost immediately and often brought what he had observed or learned there into his therapy sessions for more exploration/discussion.

Seasons in Malibu often treats public figures and usually it's not a problem for the other clients. However, David was so recognizable, his clinical team suggested he attend some private twelve-step meetings in order to further protect his anonymity.

Breaking Through!
Moments in Treatment

Individual Therapy

As he detoxed, David began to experience many feelings that drugs had kept him from feeling. Due to the death of his "mom" at a young age and recent loss of his biological mom (aunt), feelings of abandonment were at the center of several therapy sessions. Though David remembered his childhood as ideal, he also remembered being depressed at a young age, though he didn't call it depression. He considered himself lazy, evidenced by an inability to complete any project or goal he set. During his youth, a feeling he didn't understand would come over him and often cause him to hole up in his room for days. It worried his mother who said it ran in her family. He remembered his aunt, (in reality, his birth mother) living nearby with her family of four. She had these periods, too, according to his mom, who said her sister suffered like his grandmother did. They called it "the blues."

For several sessions, he could not see past his rage, but as time went on, his understanding began to shift. Initially, any comparison to his birth mother agitated him but in time, he began to wonder about her, appreciating how difficult it must have been to live nearby the baby she felt compelled to give away. As his own parenting came into view, he was ready to acknowledge how a parent can hurt a child without intending to. In one session, David said, "If you would have told me that one day, the police would escort me out of my own home, handcuffed, while my children watched, I would have called you crazy." That session proved to be a breaking through moment for him. While he made much progress during his stay, David appreciated that long term therapy would be necessary to sort through the many emotions he had about his parents, his aunt and the man who was his birth father. By the time he was discharged after a sixty-day stay, David felt hopeful that he would be able to work through these feelings.

Family Therapy

David's father was in frail health and could not travel to southern California from his Westchester, New York residence to attend family sessions. Instead, they held three tele-sessions. In them, David focused on the family secret and its impact on him. Several times, his father asked for his forgiveness. David had a hard time moving through his feelings. At one session, he became emotional. "I must've always known, that's why I've never felt very happy… Why I've never felt deserving of anything…" Though his father was visibly moved, handling his son's emotions proved challenging for the frail man. However, those sessions served as a catalyst for David. In one session that his estranged wife attended (she flew in from New York), she asked if his depression was hereditary. The likely answer was yes and that also impressed David. He said knowing that his kids could also be vulnerable fortified his desire to face whatever had to be faced. "They've already been through enough," he said during one session that caused him to cry and his estranged wife to touch his hand, the first show of affection since his admission weeks earlier.

Supportive and Complementary Treatments

Brainspotting,[1] a cutting-edge technique, locates specific "trauma" areas of the brain. Brainspotting was utilized to help David reduce the level of intensity around his emotional process of loss and abandonment. Through a series of sessions, David was able to process core traumatic experiences that were impeding his ability to function. The feelings, though still present, were not creating as much emotional activation and impulsivity as they had before David entered treatment.

Meeting TREATMENT Goals

In individual therapy sessions, David worked hard to come to terms with his past, including his sense of guilt that his success came too easily. Of the peer-based support groups, David took to the private twelve-step A.A. meetings, bonding with several other well-known actors whose addiction experiences were similar. David often expressed concern about relapse, appreciating how vulnerable he was to talking himself into just one more time. "The custody of my children was on the line and what did I do? I used." His primary therapist encouraged him to keep the memory of his last time using in his consciousness because

---

[1] Brainspotting is a new and innovative intervention focused on addressing underlying traumas, negative emotions and physical distress due to psychological pain. The "brainspot" is located through a series of directional cues by the practitioner and a pointer. The goal is to facilitate the body's limbic system to self-regulate and self-heal.

it offered the clearest example "of how addicts deceive themselves."

Individual therapy utilizing Brainspotting helped David deal with his parentage and identity issues. With time, David began to feel less sensitive about this discovery and wished he could talk to his mother and aunt. In lieu of that, David was encouraged to talk to them via journaling, which he began to do during his **Seasons** stay.

With the assistance of medication management that included anti-depressants, David was sober yet not feeling severe mood swings as he always had. He felt stronger and hoped the medication would continue to help him feel "normal".

At Discharge

David spent sixty days in treatment at **Seasons in Malibu**. At discharge, he had decided to remain in individual treatment with his **Seasons** psychologist. In addition, he continued Brainspotting treatments on an outpatient basis. David also set a goal to do whatever he had to do to regain his wife's trust and share custody of his children. She was willing to reconsider her sole custody decision provided he agree to participate in the **Seasons Aftercare Monitoring** program. The Aftercare Monitoring program protocol includes random alcohol and drug testing, ongoing case management and a central communication network so that all involved individuals are able to remain up to date on a client's sobriety. David readily agreed to allow his wife and agent access to that information whenever they requested it. Also, his agent hired a **Seasons Sober Coach** to accompany David on the set. After a year, David slowly began the reconciliation process with his wife. Although not together, the relationship improved substantially, enough for his wife to trust him with their children. Currently, they share joint custody as well as an occasional dinner date together.

IT'S THE FIRST TIME I'VE TOLD MY CHILDREN
Tallahassee Florida:Alcohol Abuse/DUI

eeks before the second anniversary of her husband's untimely death, Sarah's children gathered at her home to send the youngest sibling off to culinary school. On that evening, her two older children had mentioned their mother's "empty nest" that once was so full. Sarah dismissed their concerns and insisted she would be fine. Except by the time they left that evening, Sarah was drunk. When she reached for her son's youngest, a toddler, he squirmed from her grip. Had her son not been standing next to her, Sarah might have dropped the eighteen-month-old. The next day her daughter called. During that conversation, she told her mother that she and her brothers had some concerns about Sarah's drinking.

On the anniversary of her husband's passing, Sarah met a friend for dinner. As the valet pulled her car up, Sarah felt dizzy. Instead of waiting for the episode to pass, she proceeded to drive home, a short trip that took ten minutes in normal traffic. When she noticed lights flashing in her rearview mirror, she reduced her speed, but by then it was too late.

Sarah pulled over. On this day two years earlier, the love of her life and father of her three children had died of a cardiac arrest. The doctors had called it "The Widow Maker" and assured her that he probably felt little pain. Her thirty-three year marriage was over in one phone call. Two years later and on the day he died, Sarah got arrested for drunk driving.

After her arrest, Sarah had opportunity to call her children but couldn't make that call so she sat in jail and sobered up. As she collected her personal items at discharge, the officer informed her that she'd need a ride home. Her car had been impounded. She called her eldest son, who came to the county jail and spoke very little until they arrived at her home. Waiting for her arrival was her daughter. It was obvious she had been crying.

Sarah had always been a social drinker. She and Barry often planned vacations to include wine tasting events. Since his death, her social drinking pattern had changed. Her son told her that his wife refused to let their two children stay with her unsupervised. When she protested, he reminded her of that evening when she almost dropped his eighteen-month-old son.

She again offered an apology but it wasn't enough. "You need help, Mom," her daughter said softly. When her son added, "We're still grieving over Dad. We can't lose you, too," and began to cry, Sarah did, too.

Two weeks later, Sarah admitted herself into **Seasons in Malibu.**

Meet Sarah:
Tallahassee Florida
Alcohol Abuse/DUI

During the initial **Seasons** interview, Sarah described her drinking as social until her husband died. Sarah also said that she always drank more than he did, citing she had been a member of a wine club for years. However, during Intake, she admitted that she had been drinking quite a lot for the past several years, even before Barry's death. "We had some financial troubles that we kept from the kids," she offered. Her daughter's expression registered surprise. When a team member asked Sarah if this was the first time she had shared this information, her reply was worth noting. "It's the first time I've told my children."

Seasons Admission

Sarah arrived at **Seasons in Malibu Treatment Center** accompanied by her thirty-year-old daughter. Both mother and daughter lived in Tallahassee Florida, as did Sarah's eldest son. The youngest, a chef-in-training, attended school in Los Angeles, one reason why Sarah chose treatment at **Seasons.** Sarah was a fifty-seven-year-old white woman who was arrested two weeks before her admission to **Seasons in Malibu.** Widowed approximately two years before she was arrested for drunk driving in her home state, Sarah stated emphatically that the arrest forced her to face demons. "I don't know if I'm an alcoholic. I do know I never want to put my family through that again," she said.

Family History

Sarah always drank more than her husband Barry did but it was never a problem because he always drove. When her husband's accounting business suffered during the 2008 financial crisis, Sarah said both of them drank every evening as a way of unwinding from stress-filled days. For a few years before he died and because he had to let several employees go, Sarah would teach school daily then go to Barry's office and help with administrative work. Neither one told their children about their financial problems. When Sarah said that she believed all that stress brought on his heart attack, she started to cry. After his passing, she began to drive after drinking one or two glasses of wine. "Honestly, I didn't think much of it," said Sarah. On the night she was arrested, she drank more than usual with a friend who tended to drink a lot. "I was feeling good and sorry for myself that night," she said. "I was a bit light-headed when I got behind the wheel. Why I didn't pull over, I'll never know." Throughout the interview, Sarah kept referencing her arrest and the trauma she experienced as a result of her actions. As she spoke of that night, shame was her overriding emotion. "I was in jail. They actually handcuffed me," she repeated several times during the session. Since the arrest, she often had the same nightmare of being held prisoner in some place she couldn't escape from. The dream felt so real that when she woke up, it took her time to calm down.

Detox

Sarah hadn't had a drink since she was arrested fifteen days prior to admission. When asked if she had withdrawal symptoms, she admitted to sleeplessness and some trembling in her hands though it was not visible to staff. The **Seasons** medical team prescribed Trazadone, a mild anti-depressant that also facilitated sleep. The **Seasons** medical team also continued to assess the PTSD-like symptoms Sarah had reported, the panic-like attacks and nightmares, in order to determine if additional medication might be needed.

Community Based Support Groups

Sarah attended Alcoholics Anonymous and SMART Recovery[2] meetings during her thirty-day **Seasons** stay.

---

2 SMART Recovery is the leading self-empowering addiction recovery support group. Participants learn tools for addiction recovery based on the latest scientific research and participate in a world-wide

Perhaps because the law mandated Sarah attend A.A. meetings, she felt less comfortable in these meetings, preferring SMART Recovery. Sarah related to its focus on strength and personal responsibility.

Breaking Through! Moments in Treatment

Individual Therapy

Unresolved grief and shame were central themes in Sarah's individual therapy sessions. At Intake, when a team member observed that Sarah seemed to be editing her words, Sarah admitted that it was the first time she had spoken about financial problems in the presence of her children. She and her late husband deliberately kept them from knowing. As she became more comfortable in individual therapy sessions, she began to talk more frankly about her husband and their marriage. She said compared to her friends, she had a good marriage. "But we had problems," she offered. Her husband was a very proud man who always wanted his children to look up to him. When the

community, which includes free, self-empowering, science-based mutual help groups. The SMART Recovery 4-Point Program® helps people recover from all types of addiction and addictive behaviors, including: drug abuse, drug addiction, substance abuse, alcohol abuse, gambling addiction, cocaine addiction, prescription drug abuse, sexual addiction, and problem addiction to other substances and activities. SMART Recovery sponsors face-to-face meetings around the world, and daily online meetings.

business faltered, he took it hard. "His business depended on a robust economy that we had enjoyed for so long," said Sarah. "When it collapsed, we weren't prepared. We had taken out some loans to expand the business that we shouldn't have taken out."

As individual therapy sessions continued, it became evident that Sarah's shame about getting arrested dovetailed with her guilt regarding her husband's death. She believed the stress caused by their financial crisis caused his death. The fact that she could retire after he passed away was also a source of guilt. "His life insurance policy is why I'm financially okay today. If he were here, we probably would have sold our home to pay off the debt. We had talked about it on the very morning that he died."

Over time, Sarah was able to understand that by keeping vital details from her children, she thwarted her own grieving process. Sadness and guilt about her husband's death needed to be expressed before she could find resolution.

Family Therapy

Family therapy sessions included Sarah's youngest son, a chef apprentice in Los Angeles who had gained attention in social media for his "food as art" page on Instagram. Both her daughter and older son joined family sessions via tele-sessions. Of the many breaking through moments Sarah experienced in family therapy, the power of shame and guilt came into clear view. Sarah and Barry both came from very conservative Jewish working class homes. A commonality they shared was a desire to replicate their childhood environments for their children. Providing for and making the family proud were the pillars on which they created their family life. Admitting to error was not an option. Only with several sessions did Sarah begin to realize that false pride only increased their stress level. "We should have told the kids," she said in one session. Her youngest, always able to make her smile, said, "Did you think we'd abandon you because you made mistakes?" Before she could answer, he added "Did you abandon us when we made mistakes?" This was a breakthrough moment for Sarah. During her growing up years, making mistakes was not looked upon favorably. Sarah always did her best not to make them so her parents would be proud. In one session, Sarah connected her childhood expectations to always do the right thing with her refusal to call her children once she was in jail. Had she not needed a ride home, she might have tried to hide the arrest from them entirely. "I couldn't do it. I remember it so well. I knew I should have called them but my pride would not let me."

She recognized in sessions that both she and her husband had high expectations for all that they did. "We had accumulated so much in our years together, I think we both got caught up in thinking that we could do no wrong because everything we did--the kids, his business, my teaching career--all of it had turned out so well for us."

Her children were able to add perspective about making mistakes in their own lives. Her eldest son, most like his father, at thirty-three had high blood pressure he managed with medication. His high-pressured job wasn't as satisfying as he hoped it would be. "I wish dad would have told us," he repeated several times in one session, which proved to be pivotal for this grieving family. In subsequent sessions, each child brought up personal issues they wanted the family to know about. The youngest said that he'd been struggling with decisions about his future. The "food as art" Instagram project gave him so much more joy than cooking did. In the family's last session, he announced that the gift of his mother's hospitalization was that he had decided to quit culinary school and pursue food photography. This pleased Sarah so much she began to laugh.

Meeting TREATMENT Goals

By discharge, Sarah was a consistent contributor to SMART Recovery meetings. Sarah also took up yoga at **Seasons**. She had always wanted to but never found the time. She liked the practice very much and found a yoga center in her community to join once discharged. Grief resolution, a process Sarah gained insight about, was a cornerstone of treatment during her thirty-day stay at **Seasons in Malibu**. She began to understand that protecting her children from the truth prevented her from resolving her own grief about their father's death. Her

PTSD-like symptoms by way of nightmares abated as she grappled with the fears and feelings she had tried so hard to tamp down with alcohol.

At Discharge

Sarah's drinking had led her to "hit bottom." She appreciated that while her drinking pattern didn't seem as severe as others, it was as low as she wanted to go. For Sarah, abstinence was a small price to pay to preserve her dignity. However, she also appreciated that the stressors of being lonely could impact her resolve to remain sober. She regretted retiring because it left her with too much unscheduled time. A week before discharge, she decided to return to teaching. A remedial reading program launched at her former school offered classes for adults struggling with literacy. When she inquired about teaching positions in that program, she was told her return would be welcomed. Since Barry died, she had been socializing with a few friends who tended to drink a lot. Sarah decided to remove herself from this circle. Though she wasn't ready to date, she reconnected with a few single friends from her former school in anticipation of creating a social life to help her ward off loneliness.

After discharge, Sarah was required to attend court to resolve her legal issues with the DUI. The court was pleased to hear about her progress in treatment and recommended that she continue with the aftercare plan as well as mandated twelve-step meetings, which Sarah accepted. "Just listening to stories is such a good reminder."

One year after her probation, Sarah was finding much fulfillment in teaching adult literacy. She also decided to enroll in a yoga certification program. With the encouragement of her children, she began dating.

WE'RE GOING TO GET THROUGH THIS
Staten Island, New York: Heroin Addiction/Relapse

Jason had "slammed" many times but the last time felt different. An unfamiliar sensation hit him right before the expected rush from heroin turned into the unexpected. Without warning, he violently threw up all over himself and soon after, passed out in his own vomit. His friend, about to shoot up what Jason had injected, didn't like what he saw. Jason's complexion had turned muddy gray; so instead, his friend called 911 but split before the paramedics and police arrived at the Staten Island warehouse that had become Jason's second home.

When he woke up later in the hospital room, Jason told his mother he remembered the paramedics pounding on his chest. He told her he knew what was happening to him. He knew he was dying and he wanted to die. When the paramedics brought him back, he remembered feeling angry.

Jason was transferred to a medical unit to monitor a heart arrhythmia that couldn't be stabilized in the E.R. Later that day, the physician entered Jason's room and told him and his parents that tainted smack was probably why his heartbeat had become dangerously irregular. "You didn't almost die from heroin, you almost died from poison you injected. We think it's the kind used commercially to kill rats but we won't know until the labs come back. This happens often so if you decide you want to keep shooting up," he paused long enough to extend his arm toward Jason's parents, "expect this not to end well for you or for them. " He scribbled his name on Jason's discharge papers, ripped a copy off, handed it to Jason's dad and left the room. Jason's mother broke down. His dad did, too. Jason immediately apologized because by then, he knew that's what he should do. He also knew it fell on deaf ears, the by-product of too many apologies without any change.

His dad grabbed his hand. He'd found a treatment facility across the country and as he began to describe **Seasons in Malibu**, Jason pulled his hand away. "We've been down this road too many times. Give it up, Dad. Nothing's gonna help. You heard him. This is not going to end well so give up!"

Jason's words had a quieting effect on his dad who didn't reply for a moment. When he did, he had command of his voice. "Had my brother given up on me, I wouldn't be standing here, Jason. You know that. You've got nothing to lose so I'm asking you to give it a shot. Besides, this center has great ocean views."

As dim as hope could get, Jason's dad always had the ability to make his son laugh. When he saw Jason smile slightly, he read that as the first sign of hope since receiving that call to get to the hospital quick because his son might be dying.

Meet Jason:
Staten Island, NY
Heroin Addiction/Multiple Hospitalizations

Jason is a twenty-five year old heroin addict treated in two different facilities prior to entering **Seasons in Malibu**. His first admission was at age eighteen. His drug of choice--then and now--heroin. He said from the first taste of heroin, he was hooked.

Jason is the oldest of three children. Though his parents were raised in a working class neighborhood in Staten Island, soon after his birth, Jason's family-owned trash disposal company rapidly grew. By the time Jason's youngest sister was born, his family had become well off financially.

Jason's parents divorced when Jason had just turned ten. His father said it was due to his own alcoholism and unpredictable behavior. For the next few years, his dad was rarely around. During this time, his mom also became a heavy drinker. Many days, Jason would return home from school to be told by their housekeeper that his mother was ill and confined to her room. He was never allowed in her room, though he often heard her yelling and throwing things. Sometimes the kids would be left solely in the care of their housekeeper, a kind woman Jason said, who spoke very little English.

When he was eleven, his mother attempted to drive while drunk but Jason grabbed the keys. She became incensed, raged on him in front of his younger sisters and demanded the keys. He would not give them to her; instead, he bolted and did not return home for several hours. He described this as his first attempt at running away. By the time Jason was thirteen, he was running away from home often, attending raves and crashing at homes of friends whose parents, like his, were inattentive. He also began using drugs: beer and pot mostly. His mother was on several prescription sedatives. He began stealing from her medicine cabinet. With so many prescription bottles, she never noticed.

When Jason was sixteen, his dad came back into his family to care for his mother. He had been sober for over a year and told his children that he needed to make up for the time lost. Except by then, Jason had an alcohol and prescription drug habit and did not want anything to do with his father. Jason's mother was admitted into an addiction treatment center, where she remained for 30 days. She came home, relapsed within a year, returned to the center and spent another three months in treatment. At Jason's admission, both parents were sober, though Jason's father described his wife as "emotionally not well" which was why she could not accompany them to **Seasons**.

Seasons Admission

Jason was admitted to **Seasons** accompanied by his father and younger sister who attended a university in southern California. He was very thin and his hands visibly shook. His dad was kind toward him as was his sister who kept repeating, "We're going to get through this." Jason spoke little throughout the Intake interview though he was frank about his view of the future. He saw himself as hopelessly addicted to heroin. His dad kept bringing up his own addiction but Jason discounted alcoholism stating it was nothing compared to heroin addiction. Jason's dad shared with the team his own story. He said that one of the mistakes he probably made was not showing his kids his darkest days. "If I had, he wouldn't think alcoholism is a walk in the park, I'll tell you that," he said and though he attempted to smile, he welled up. "I walked out on my family and ended up in jail twice. Had my brothers not covered my back, I would have lost the family business." His eldest brother, a recovering alcoholic, was a member of A.A. "He told me if I didn't get help, he'd have to take legal action to protect the business from me."

Jason's sister said their mother believed her son's addiction was her fault. When Jason was asked to respond, all he said was that she was troubled and took it out on him. "She more than took it out on you, Jason. You were the only one protecting us and she was cruel when she was drunk," said his sister. Though his mother had worked hard to stay sober, she continued to struggle. "You should know this," Jason's dad said to the **Seasons** team. Directing his words to his children, he said, "I'll carry that with me for the rest of my life, too." He stopped speaking though his gaze remained on his kids. "You move forward. You thank God you're given another chance and you move forward. I can't change my past. I can only make sure that today I won't repeat it, and today, I won't. That's going to have to be good enough for you too, Jason, one day at a time."

Jason's younger sister planned to attend weekly family therapy sessions. His youngest sister lived in New York and made a commitment to attend some family therapy sessions and promised, via a telephone conversation during **Seasons** Intake, to do her best to bring their mom with her. When Jason was asked how he felt about his mom participating in treatment, he took some time responding before offering that it might help. His dad patted Jason's knee. "We'll get her here, son" he said.

Family History

Jason's ethnic background included Italian on his mother's side and Irish on his father's side. On both sides, heavy drinking was always included in any family activity. Jason remembered getting sips of beer at a very young age, just as all of his cousins did. His father also drank heavily throughout his high school years, enough to keep him from playing football, a game Jason's grandfather played in high school and expected his son to play, too. During the **Seasons** Intake, Jason's dad said that his father used to beat him every time he caught him drinking. "One time he fractured my cheekbone," his dad said softly.

Jason was first hospitalized for heroin addiction when he was eighteen and only weeks after graduating high school. He was discharged in time to begin fall semester of his freshman year at a state university, but within three weeks he was expelled for selling drugs on campus. His father was livid and kicked him out of the house. For the next few years, they had very little contact. During this period of time, Jason overdosed, and again, a friend found him unconscious and called 911. Within twenty-four hours, Jason was admitted into the second facility for heroin addiction. He was twenty-two. He remained in treatment for two months and when he was discharged, he moved back home and began working in the family business. He attended Narcotics Anonymous (N.A.) meetings though his dad said he did not relate to N.A. members the way he and his brother (Jason's uncle) related to A.A. He also became involved with a girl and for a while, Jason felt "almost normal" he said during **Seasons'** Intake. Several weeks before admission, Jason's girlfriend ended the relationship. He was devastated but okay until he found out that she had been cheating on him with his former best friend from grammar school, a friend who had distanced himself in high school due to Jason's drug problems. Once Jason found this out, he left home and again returned to the streets. His only family contact was when he needed money deposited into his checking account. His dad always obliged, fearing that if he didn't, he would never see his son again.

Detox

Opioid detox protocols are typically managed through a series of monitored and specific tapers. Although the evidence supports that individuals rarely die from an opiate detox—unlike an alcohol detox or benzodiazepine detox, both of which are significantly more risky without monitoring—still, the effects of going through heroin withdrawal can be very uncomfortable. As a way of managing that discomfort, the medical team ensures a measured taper protocol, typically of a partial opiate agonist such as Suboxone. This medication mimics the effects of the opiate without the level of addictive qualities and concerns for misuse. Additionally, it facilitates increased comfort so the client can participate in treatment. Jason had a one-week taper of Suboxone. The benefits of this M.D.-monitored withdrawal include a high level of oversight and the ability to immediately make medication adjustments when/if necessary. In the event that the medical team might decide to add psychotropic drugs to his treatment plan, a metabolic/genetic test was ordered to determine which drugs might work best and how Jason's body would likely respond.

Community Based Support Groups

Seasons offers multiple recovery models; due to his family's success with twelve-step programs and his need to feel nurtured by a community, Narcotics Anonymous seemed to be a good fit. Jason embraced N.A. meetings almost immediately. He said members reminded him daily of an addict's ability to deny. "I need to hear that every day," Jason said. "That's my biggest hurdle to sobriety—denying the consequences of using one more time."

Breaking Through! Moments in Treatment

Individual Therapy

Jason did not try to hide his pessimism about treatment. During initial sessions, he consistently challenged his therapist about treatments he'd been exposed to. None of them worked. As Jason detoxed, his therapist spent most of these sessions listening to him discuss how hard life was for him. "Heroin is not a drug you walk away from," was the mantra he maintained. At one session, his therapist asked if he took pride in knowing that he could not walk away. "You know, that you've got an addiction that only a select few get to have," said his therapist. Jason took time answering. "Because I'm so special," he replied as a slight smile emerged. This session proved to be a breaking through moment for Jason who began to talk about how scared he was that he wouldn't be able to remain sober—the same fear he held for his mother.

Individual sessions tapped into feelings centered on his early teen years. He had guilt about running away when his little sisters needed him to stay home. His guilt also centered on his mom's drinking. "I'd come home after a few days and she'd compare me to my dad, accuse me of being just like him, which usually sent me out the door again," he said.

Family Therapy

Jason and his father participated in weekly family therapy sessions via telephone. In the initial session, Jason's father shared a vivid overview of their family's addiction patterns. On both sides, addictions to alcohol, prescription pills and/or tobacco ran through the generations. The working class on Staten Island worked hard and played hard according to Jason's father; their families were no exception. There was also family evidence of depression, especially on his mother's side. If she didn't maintain a therapeutic level of medication used to treat her depression, the resulting highs and lows tended to trigger her drinking.

His dad took ownership for Jason's traumatic childhood. He pleaded with Jason to talk about it, believing

Jason had to revisit all of it before he could move on. He shared much of his own story, parts of which were very difficult for him to share with his son. "I believe it's in our genes and all of us have to accept this: me, you, your sisters and your mother. My father was a mean drunk. When he was sober, I adored the guy but he wasn't sober much and I took it personally. I always felt like we weren't good enough to be sober for and then what did I do? I did the same goddamn thing to my kids." He broke down often during the first several sessions, behavior Jason had not witnessed. In family therapy sessions at Jason's previous treatment centers, his father tended to remain angry. When the **Seasons** therapist asked his dad why he didn't present his anger in these sessions, he replied that over time, he realized his anger was more about himself and the impact his addiction had on his family; the real fear was about his family never being whole. This was pivotal for Jason because it finally, and for the first time, helped him understand his father.

Meeting TREATMENT Goals

The work Jason was able to do in family therapy sessions during his ninety-day stay was positively impacted by his father's contributions. Jason developed a solid understanding of how much addiction impacted his entire family, from his grandfather to his uncles, to his dad and his mom. **Seasons** recommended a long-term sober living environment post-discharge and Jason readily agreed. His dad encouraged him to find a center on the east coast so he could visit. However, Jason had visited a sober living environment not far from **Seasons in Malibu**. He told his dad he thought staying in California was better for him. His dad agreed.

At Discharge

Jason left **Seasons in Malibu** for a sober living center located in Southern California. At discharge, he had already attended several N.A. meetings near his new dwelling and expressed positive feelings about the people he met. Jason's **Seasons** family therapy sessions continued post-discharge via tele-sessions. Jason expressed interest in working on issues related to his mom, which his therapist supported. However, due to Jason's relapse history, his therapist suggested they remain focused on sobriety, a suggestion Jason's dad heartily supported. In time, the goal was to hold consistent family therapy sessions with all members present. And in time, they did.

SHERIFF JACK, FACING FEARS
San Bernardino, California: PTSD w/ Poly-Drug Abuse, Alcohol and Sedatives

"Cops get killed. You know that going in," said Jack, a forty-two-year-old deputy sheriff during his **Seasons** Intake. "But I can't shake it and I don't know that I ever will." Had Jack's partner not stopped by his house that afternoon, Jack would be dead. He had decided to die rather than live with the panic, the night terrors and all the rest that followed the incident at work that caused him to turn to alcohol and prescription drugs just to get through each day.

"It's part of the job," he repeated often during Intake, his wife of twenty years at his side. They had two children and a marriage that was happy until this incident changed all that. "He became someone else," Jack's wife said. He agreed.

The incident, an arrest on the street that went terribly wrong, resulted in the death of the perpetrator, but not before he pointed a shotgun at Jack's face from a distance of less than ten feet. That incident sent Jack spinning out of control with nightmares, day terrors and panic attacks, enough to be hospitalized, once involuntarily by his wife who feared he would *harm himself. As much as he tried to get through it, the terrors became worse. His drinking and prescription drug taking did, too, which only heightened symptoms.*

Jack recalled the day he decided enough was enough. He kept his intentions private except for one conversation he had with his partner, an officer he had shared a car with for five years. Later, his partner said that Jack just didn't sound right. He knew Jack was having a tough time so on the day they spoke by phone, he swung by the house before going to work and found Jack hanging from a tree in the backyard. He cut him down and administered mouth-to-mouth. Jack responded and he called 911.

"I guess it wasn't my time," Jack said in the interview. His wife grabbed his hand and began to cry. He welled up, too, as he patted hers.

Meet Jack:
San Bernardino, California
PTSD w/Poly-Drug Abuse, Alcohol and Sedatives

Jack T. from San Bernardino, California, sought treatment at **Seasons in Malibu** three months after discharge from another facility where his wife had him admitted involuntarily on a 5150 Hold because she feared he was planning to take his life. The seventy-two hour hold is used to determine a person's "harm to self or others" potential. Once the hold expired and the court determined he was no longer a danger to himself, Jack decided to remain in treatment at the facility and was transferred to a lower level of care unit. By his account, very little treatment was offered. "They treated me with drugs. That pretty much was it," said Jack at Intake. "I never felt emotionally better and I was there for almost a month." After discharge, his PTSD symptoms intensified, only this time his wife insisted they find the right treatment center. **Seasons in Malibu** is known for its treatment of trauma, implementing several therapeutic tools specifically aimed at management of PTSD symptoms: rage, depression, night terrors, panic attacks, insomnia and haunting images plague most suffering from Post-Traumatic Stress Disorder, PTSD. Though he wanted help, Jack doubted any would be found. When his wife read about **Seasons'** trauma work posted on the website, she insisted they make contact. They called even though Jack assumed their insurance would not cover the **Seasons in Malibu** treatment program. He led with that assumption when they made contact. Though his wife offered some information, she told the Admission Director that until they heard about insurance coverage, her husband didn't want to spend too much time by phone offering his history. A thorough review of their policy revealed that Jack's insurance did cover treatment. **Seasons'** chief financial officer personally called Jack to deliver the good news. Jack made an appointment to be admitted the following day.

Seasons Admission

A sense of urgency from Jack's wife was noted during Intake. A **Seasons** clinician shared this observation and asked for confirmation. She was quite frank, explaining to the team that she had known her husband since high school. Because of their history, she felt certain that the next time he felt the kind of desperation he felt on that day, Jack would succeed in killing himself. "He had that planned out," she said. "The boys and I had just left for the weekend. He wasn't quite ready, but at some point he will be because he can't live like this."

Jack was the eldest in a family of four children: two brothers and one sister born several years after her three brothers' births. His dad served in the military and was pleased when Jack decided to join the Sheriff's department after his own discharge from military service. His wife used the word "macho" to describe Jack's dad and said that though she liked him, she also had issues with his male bravado, especially after her sons were born. "When they were still toddlers, he'd tell them 'boys don't cry' if they fell down and hurt themselves. I had to lay down some ground rules." Jack confirmed that he was raised to be tough and described his dad as "a product of his time." His sister came much later and the message to protect her was reinforced consistently by their father. "And we always did," Jack said. When asked about his expectations for his own sons, Jack looked like he didn't understand the question. "Would you like either one of your boys to be a police officer?" Jack's head shook vigorously. "There's got to be a better way for them to make a living," he said.

Based on Jack's history and symptoms presented, the Clinical Director suggested that Jack could benefit from a comprehensive psychological evaluation.[3] **Seasons** ordered a battery of psychological testing to tease out specific symptoms of trauma Jack was sensitive to. The plan included reviewing test results with Jack and developing a treatment plan based on the psychological "triggers" that testing revealed.

Family History

Jack and Sally, parents of two teenage boys, were high school sweethearts who enjoyed a happy marriage. Acknowledging they had weathered storms, it was always together. The incident at work changed all that. Jack withdrew and when he did engage, he was often hostile. "Never in our twenty-year marriage have I ever been

---

3 Psychological evaluations are quantifiable tools and assessments that provide evidence for an individual's underlying emotional distress.

afraid of Jack," said his wife to the clinical psychologist at the Intake interview. Jack had displayed little emotion during the interview until his wife mentioned her fear. He became visibly agitated. The **Seasons** clinician asked him to respond. He struggled and was encouraged to find words. In a quiet voice Jack said, "I promise you I will kill myself before I ever hurt my family."

Jack had a solid family support system in place: his wife and two sons. He also had a strong support system at the Sheriff's department, describing his partner and his family as "our family."

Jack's wife committed to attend all family therapy sessions and agreed their sons would be involved when appropriate. Several times during the first meeting, she referred to Jack's "sense of pride," the term she used to describe his reaction to the incident at work that almost claimed his life. He didn't expect to react the way he did because, as he said repeatedly, "It's part of the job." His reaction to the threat made him feel less of a man. His wife said he felt like a failure. She talked about their sons and how Jack had always been a hero to them. He enjoyed his job as a sheriff and until this incident, never expressed fear about being in the department. Since the incident, he found it difficult to be around the boys and often made excuses for not attending their sports events. The truth was, he was fearful of open spaces, just one of many PTSD symptoms Jack tried to manage with alcohol and seda-tives. His "pride" kept him from being honest with his sons. Not knowing how to deal with their dad (who had never missed games), they tended to avoid him when he was home.

Detox

From the time he left the initial treatment center to his admission at **Seasons** three months later, Jack had self-medicated with alcohol and Xanax, frequently to the point of blacking out. He was slightly tremulous but did not have complaints of withdrawal except for insomnia, which had plagued him since the incident at work first triggered the severe PTSD. He was placed on a mild detox taper protocol to facilitate any discomfort and potential medical complications.

Community Based Support Groups

Because of his prior hospitalization where the only treatment he received was via twelve-step meetings (a.k.a. Alcoholics Anonymous), Jack was not open to attending them. **Seasons in Malibu** offers a broad range of relevant recovery and therapeutic groups. Once he made some friends, Jack was encouraged by them to try SMART Recovery (Self-Management and Recovery Training) meetings. A **Seasons** client described it as "an abstinence program that puts you in control." Jack liked the sound of that and from the first meeting, he felt like he fit in. SMART Recovery meetings became a staple in Jack's routine. His involvement in these meetings helped him feel like he was in charge. "I know it's not going to be easy but I need to feel like I can lick this." Jack said. SMART Recovery members must be willing to own behavior and understand why it developed initially, a viewpoint Jack shared. "Not everyone becomes a drunk to cope with trauma," Jack said during one SMART Recovery session. "I've got to remember this when I leave here."

Breaking Through! Moments in Treatment

Individual Therapy

Jack initially met with a **Seasons** psychiatrist whose prior experience in the military impressed him. Whenever Jack spoke, he directed his words either to his wife or to this psychiatrist sitting across from him. Once admitted and due to his multiple trauma symptoms, the Intake psychiatrist recommended that **Seasons'** Clinical Director become Jack's primary therapist, his expertise in EMDR,[4] Eye Movement Desensitization and Reprocessing, the reason why. EMDR, an integrative psychotherapy approach

---

4 EMDR, Eye Movement Desensitization and Reprocessing, is an integrative psychotherapy approach proven effective for the treatment of trauma. The long-term goal, desensitization, is ongoing and tools needed to address the trauma are taught in EMDR sessions conducted by a certified EMDR therapist.

for the treatment of trauma is used quite effectively at **Seasons**.

The Clinical Director became Jack's primary therapist. During initial sessions, the topic of "what it means to be a man in our society" was a major focus. In time and with assistance via EMDR tools, Jack was able to identify early learning patterns that were set by his father, and contrast them with his own beliefs about being a man. The goal of EMDR Therapy is to process the experiences that are causing problems, and to include new experiences that are needed for full health. "Processing" means setting up a learning state that will allow experiences that are causing problems to be digested and stored appropriately in memory. Until he entered **Seasons in Malibu**, neither Jack nor his wife had any idea that PTSD had sophisticated treatments specifically designed for management/ care of this collection of post-trauma symptoms, ranging from mild to severe. Jack's almost fatal suicide attempt put him in the severe category.

The psychological testing results and EMDR-focused therapy sessions helped give Jack a "visual" road back to wellness, an image that gave him incentive to stick with the traumatic feelings emerging in sessions—difficult feelings necessary to face and feel before desensitization can occur. An EMDR tenet, that negative emotions, feelings and behaviors are generally caused by unresolved earlier experiences pushing the person in the wrong direction, made so much sense to Jack. His father's rigid view of acceptable male behavior collided with Jack's response to his own near-death experience. Jack came to realize that in addition to feeling a fear such as he had never felt before, he also felt much shame because he had not lived up to his father's view of manhood. Those opposing emotions had to be resolved. As Jack continued to explore this in individual therapy sessions, he made great strides in defining himself as separate from his father. If he didn't want his sons to carry that distorted image of manhood into their futures, he had to resolve the conflict and make peace with who he was: a man who did not carry his father's narrow expectations of how males should behave.

Jack developed a strong connection to the men's group offered at **Seasons.** The opportunity to listen to and share feelings with other males was such a source of comfort. Many men told similar stories about their fathers and how those messages shaped their ability to manage their own emotions. This normalized Jack's experience and made him feel much less alone.

Family Therapy

From the first family therapy session, it became clear that Jack felt like a failure at many levels. Though intellectually he understood why he had dropped out and began drinking to blackout stage, he had trouble accepting this behavior until he gained insights in treatment, breaking through-like moments that centered on his view of manhood. His wife offered that several times, usually when he was quite inebriated, he'd profusely apologize for being a weakling, cry and then apologize for doing that.

Family therapy did not have to focus on faulty communication patterns because this couple clearly heard each other. As Jack began to feel stronger, he brought up his wife's lingering fear about the boys. "I notice she's ready to intervene when they're visiting, like maybe she thinks I'm going to start yelling." His wife confirmed Jack's suspicion, adding that she and boys had been going through their own version of PTSD. "So can you blame me for being overprotective now, Jack?" she asked in one meeting. He smiled and nodded in agreement. Her protectiveness was the focus of several therapy sessions, as behavior that became necessary when Jack began to rage. The boys participated in several sessions, and with support, both were able to verbalize sadness about what had happened to their dad. When the older son also expressed hope that his dad was getting better, the younger son said, "Yea Dad, you look better." Everyone laughed.

Meeting TREATMENT Goals

By the time Jack was ready for discharge, he no longer felt ashamed of his behaviors. Jack embraced EMDR and SMART Recovery; these two therapeutic modalities, along with intensive one-on-one therapy, became the cornerstones of his treatment. He appreciated learning about triggers. He also had a solid understanding of the desensitization techniques employed in treatment to defuse potentially dangerous emotional situations set off by these internal and deeply rooted triggers. By the time he left, he was implementing these techniques independent of his primary therapist.

As discharge approached, Jack was asked about returning to street duty at the Sheriff's department. He said he wanted to return because he missed his colleagues in the department, especially his partner. He felt equipped to handle stressors with his new tools and support systems. Unlike his last discharge, Jack left feeling "whole" again. For some clients, the image of empowerment fosters this feeling. Jack was one of these clients.

At Discharge

At discharge, Jack was prescribed no medication except a sleeping aid to take on "as needed" basis. SMART Recovery meetings were found near his home and with the help of Jack's Case Manager, they found a therapist in Jack's community trained in EMDR. Jack scheduled his first session before he left **Seasons**. The Sheriff's Department welcomed Jack back when he was ready and three weeks after discharge, Jack returned to work full-time. Six weeks after he returned to work, Jack called **Seasons**' Clinical Director. His insomnia had returned and he was afraid to take any sleeping pills. "I'm afraid if I take one, I'll take them all," Jack told him. Even though EMDR tools helped, he noticed an escalation in symptoms. "I want to nip this in the bud before it gets worse," he said. After consulting with Jack's current therapist, it was agreed that Jack could benefit from returning to **Seasons** for some intensive outpatient sessions.

Post-Discharge... More Breaking Through!

Jack's return to **Seasons** included several sessions with both his primary therapist and relevant groups. The focus of these back-to-back sessions centered on Jack's decision to return to street patrol. He realized it was the wrong decision. "Maybe it was the last of my dad's influence talking in my head." Jack asked for a reassignment within the department that did not require street patrol. He continued EMDR individual therapy weekly and became very active in SMART Recovery meetings both online and in his community. One year after discharge, and with the support of the Sheriff's Department, he implemented a PTSD awareness program for law enforcement officers in his county.

LIVE FAST, DIE YOUNG
Atlanta Georgia: Chronic Opiate/Heroin Abuse

When the older brother of well-known rapper "Vicious T" ("Tyrone") watched him fall off the stage before a capacity crowd in a world-renowned venue, he made up his mind. If Tyrone didn't get help, some serious help, he would leave the band and take everybody with him.

In the past year, Tyrone had fallen down on stage twice and fallen off three times during a performance. One incident resulted in a broken ankle that forced Tyrone to cancel several concerts. Up until the last fall, Tyrone's publicity team was able to keep the truth from the public regarding his drug addiction. The last fall not only made tabloid news, the story ran on several daily news shows and in many newspapers around the country.

In the **Seasons In Malibu** Intake interview, this superstar's older brother sat directly across from Tyrone and repeated words spoken the morning after the latest incident on stage hit tabloid news outlets.

---

56   Breaking Through! Stories of Hope & Recovery

"I said it straight up then and meant every word. If you think I'm going to stand by and watch you kill yourself right in front of me…" He paused and looked away. After a moment, **Seasons'** Intake clinician encouraged him to continue. Locking his gaze on Tyrone, his brother did. "That just ain't gonna happen, baby brother. You wanna kill yourself? You'll have to do that without me. I'm done covering for you and done with you period if you don't stop all this crazy drugging. Done!"

Meet Tyrone:
Atlanta, Georgia
Poly-Substance Abuse/Previous Hospitalizations

Tyrone was a thirty-four-year-old African American male rap artist. His love for this musical expression collided with his drug abuse and at age twenty-four, Tyrone almost died of a heroin overdose. The experience scared him enough to quit that drug, which he did for the next eight years.

At age thirty-two, Tyrone won his first Grammy Award and soon after that, relatives he hadn't heard from began reconnecting, including his estranged father. Within months of their reunion, Tyrone began using opiates again that included heroin and Vicodin.

Seasons Admission

Tyrone's older brother and band member brought Tyrone to **Seasons in Malibu**. The family viewed this intervention and treatment as a last-ditch effort. His brother stated quite clearly that after Tyrone's last public display of his addiction, blacking out and falling off stage, the scene witnessed by almost 20,000 fans, he would not continue playing in the band. "I walked away from our old man and never looked back so don't you think I can't do that with you if I have to. And I'm taking our mother with me cause she's suffered enough."

Family History

Tyrone lived in Atlanta, Georgia where his three young children also resided. Each child had a different mother and though none of these relationships was serious, Tyrone wanted to do right by his kids. He knew the chronic chaos caused by his addictions prevented him from being the kind of father he said he wanted to be. In the **Seasons in Malibu** Intake interview, Tyrone often brought up the role of father. He had recently reunited with his own father, a man addicted to many drugs for much of his life. According to Tyrone's brother and mother, this reunion triggered Tyrone's return to heroin abuse. Shortly after reuniting, Tyrone realized that his father's main reason for reconnecting was to benefit from Tyrone's new wealth, a realization that triggered his relapse. Once Tyrone's health was again compromised through poly-opiate use, he was unable to set a very necessary boundary with his father even though his mother and brother consistently encouraged him to do so.

Tyrone's family structure is one familiar to people living below the poverty level. He was raised in the New York City projects by his mother, a woman with four children who worked two jobs to support them once Tyrone's father left the family. He described his mother as "an amazing woman." Like many African American males of his generation, male role models were not as prevalent as the "modeling" provided by the many gangs that controlled his neighborhood. As a child, he was small in stature and often ridiculed for his diminutive size and inability to read well. Walking down the street invited the name-calling; words like "midget" and "dumb shit" were screamed at him often. He did not know that he suffered from ADHD, a cognitive disorder that prevented him from learning like other children. He was a constant target for bullies at school. Throughout his grammar school years, his small size and inability to read caused him to feel much shame.

Tyrone's father was physically and emotionally abusive. With regularity, he would use alcohol and/or drugs in front of him and then beat Tyrone's mother and the children. When he left, Tyrone remembers feeling relief, especially for his mother, who no longer had to endure his father's beatings. But life was very difficult and the influence of street life made its way into Tyrone's home. At the same time he began connecting to the music of his environment, rap music, he began using drugs. Tyrone's need to express himself found an outlet in rap music, a language he understood.

Detox

After his initial medically supervised detox, Tyrone was evaluated to assess the severity of his learning disorder. Tyrone's self-image regarding his intelligence was impacted by his poor reading skills. After appropriate neuropsychological testing was administered, **Seasons** was able to determine that his IQ was above average and his limitations in learning were due to untreated Attention Deficit Disorder.

Breaking Through!
Moments In Treatment

Individual Therapy

The dynamics in Tyrone's young life are familiar to minority groups living below the poverty level in northern urban cities where federal housing once dominated neighborhoods. The challenge for the treatment team included understanding the dynamics of children born into poverty who later on have larger-than-life success. Research suggests that young black men born into these conditions historically don't live a long life, which explained the "live fast, die young" aura projected by many rap artists. The infusion of success and money doesn't necessarily change this mindset formed in early life so it becomes the work of the artist to shift his/her viewpoint. At admission, it was clear that Tyrone wanted to try. He wanted to enjoy his success. He wanted to be a better son, brother, father and man. Individual one-on-one therapy focused on this desire to become the kind of father he didn't have. The fear that he would not be able to provide what he didn't experience lessened with time. Tyrone began to appreciate that unlike his father, he wanted to learn how to become a better man. Issues explored centered on Tyrone's early life; trauma was a major theme. Utilizing a cognitive-behavioral approach, Tyrone was able to examine specific traumatic childhood events and recognize some behaviors he had adopted to cope with these traumas, behaviors that included reliance on drugs to change the way he felt. In time, Tyrone was able to identify childhood traumas and the effect of those traumas on his behavior. He was able to appreciate the choices he had made to cope with his childhood image of himself as "less than"—choices that eventually led to his addictions.

Family Therapy

Tyrone's mother was quite upset that Tyrone had allowed his father to re-enter his life. In family therapy sessions, a review of early life traumas that included his father's abuse helped both Tyrone and his mother identify behaviors that she implemented to protect him as a young child. Those behaviors were difficult for his mother to relinquish even though Tyrone was no longer a child. As treatment progressed, Tyrone heard his mother's fear about following in his father's footsteps. With some therapeutic structure provided in sessions, he was also able to set some boundaries on her "possessiveness"—the word he used to describe her behavior toward him.

Group Therapy

Tyrone utilized group, specifically a family systems-based group, to work out some issues with his father. **Seasons** family systems groups focus on ways individuals are influenced by their active family roles, traumas and ongoing patterns, all of which can contribute to unhealthy interactions. Though he seemed to be in touch with his anger regarding his father's lack of parenting and also had no problem expressing his rage in lyrics, Tyrone had a much harder time expressing his anger off-stage. Tyrone did have access to his own fear that he wouldn't be there for his kids if he continued living an addict's life. The **Seasons** team helped him connect his anger at his dad's abandonment with his own fear of abandoning his children. Identifying behavioral patterns from his childhood helped Tyrone identify those behaviors that threatened his wellbeing as an adult. Taking drugs to avoid feelings was what his dad did, he did, and in all likelihood what one or all his children would likely do if he didn't break this cycle.

In group, as in all therapeutic interventions, the psychologist kept the focus on Tyrone's last relapse, the one that led him to this **Seasons** admission. He stated with certainty that his use of heroin was related to the pain he felt once he realized that his father only came back to enjoy his financial success. The group reinforced his insight regarding this awareness and encouraged him to continue the work he was doing therapeutically.

Supportive and Complementary Treatments

Tyrone needed daily time to exercise. He also needed time to practice/compose at his keyboard, which **Seasons** allowed and encouraged during his stay. Music had always been the avenue into his feelings. In his sixty-day inpatient treatment, Tyrone's ability to identify and express feelings, especially negative feelings, improved significantly.

Financial planning/guidance: With his case manager present, Tyrone's brother briefed him on his financial portfolio, an overview Tyrone tracked well. As Tyrone moved closer to discharge, the team added several financial education sessions to his treatment plan. Though he tended to be good-natured about all the money he made but didn't keep, due in part to his own neglect, Tyrone wanted to secure a future for his children. The decision was made to bring in a financial coach to help Tyrone manage his money.

Legal Counsel: A family law specialist gave Tyrone guidance regarding his obligations to his children, visitation rights, etc. Unfortunately, the mothers of his children often asked him for lots of money and when he got fed up with the amount he was giving one, he stopped giving to all. The family law attorneys helped Tyrone clear up his legal issues and avoid any future conflicts.

At Discharge

Seasons in Malibu's discharge plan begins at admission. In Tyrone's case, he left with new tools to navigate through challenges bound to greet this very successful performer once he returned to his real world. Tyrone discharged with a commitment to a ninety-day outpatient plan that included the following:

Tyrone wanted to continue work as an outpatient; particularly he wanted to explore mother-son, brother-brother and his fathering roles. The **Seasons** family therapy team found a family therapy practice in Atlanta that worked with the **Seasons** team through Tyrone's transition from in-patient to outpatient. Since he traveled to LA with regularity, Tyrone asked to remain in individual therapy with his **Seasons** therapist. On the weeks he wasn't in LA, he agreed to complete the given assignments and tasks offered by his one-on-one therapist. At time of discharge, Tyrone's father refused to join his son in therapy, stating, "I don't need no Dr. Phil." Tyrone informed him that if he ever changed his mind, the door was open.

A sober companion was hired to travel with his band for ninety-days post discharge. Sober companions are individuals that facilitate ongoing sobriety for clients. They serve as facilitators in order to ease the compulsions and burdens of addiction. Most companions are also in recovery. Tyrone committed to attend A.A./N.A. meetings at home and on the road. His personal attorney/financial mentor was hired to implement protection of Tyrone's assets from his children's mothers as well as to provide monthly support for each child. A custodial agreement that included consistent visitation rights so he could reunite with his children was drafted and signed by all parties. The agreement included a provision to bring his kids on the road once they were old enough.

Tyrone left **Seasons in Malibu** equipped with coping skills he did not have access to prior to his admission for poly-drug abuse. His goal at discharge was to continue to learn how to live a sober life for himself and for his kids.

Three years post-discharge, Tyrone continues to live a sober life.

WHEN? I WANT IT NOW!
Northern California: Alcohol Poisoning/Alcohol Abuse

When Jenevieve woke up at three in the morning, lying in her own vomit on the floor of her bedroom suite, it wasn't the first time this sixty-three-year-old senior Silicon Valley executive had blacked out from drinking. It wasn't the first time she had reached for the vodka bottle nearby and put it to her lips, desperate to rid herself of the pain. She vaguely recalled not taking a drink, or at least she didn't think she did. She recalled feeling a panic like she had never felt before. "I honestly thought I was going to die right there on the floor of my bedroom." Not only did she believe she was dying, Jenevieve believed she was powerless to do anything about it. That was her last recollection.

Jenevieve didn't recall the paramedics in her condominium. She did remember waking up in the emergency room with her son, who at the time was a medical intern, on one side and her family physician on the other. She did remember her family physician leaning over her bed, his face within inches of hers. "You will be dead in six months, Jen, maybe sooner, if *you don't stop."* She remembered the sounds of sadness coming from her son. *"He was sobbing,"* she said softly as she continued recalling the incident that brought her to the E.R. that night. She remembered her family physician telling her that she may have already caused irreparable damage to her brain and nervous system. *"After some testing, we'll know more,"* he said and then left the room.

How does a woman who climbed up from her working class background to the top of corporate America find herself at death's door due to her inability to stop drinking? Jenevieve had no answer. *"I thought I did everything right,"* she said during her first consultation with **Seasons** staff. *"I wanted to make everyone proud of me,"* she offered. *"Now look at me. I could be dying from this and I don't even know how it happened."*

Meet Jenevieve:
Northern California
Alcohol Dependence with
Damaging Neurological Effects

Jenevieve was a sixty–three-year-old executive living the American dream. Her roots were working class and the message from her parents, her dad especially, heard since childhood, was constant: If you work really hard, your dreams can come true. She did. The third of three children, Jenevieve entered Information Technology as a young woman and climbed the ladder until she became CEO of a prominent Silicon Valley company where she remained for fourteen years. Six months before her **Seasons** admission, Jenevieve entered the monthly board meeting where the board of directors asked her to step down from her CEO duties. She was stunned, the request devastating. Since her youth, Jen's identity was intertwined with her professional status. She worked harder than anyone she knew and had sacrificed much to reach the top of corporate America. With the exception of her son, an MD/intern at the time of her **Seasons** admission, Jenevieve had no close relationships. Her only friends were connected to her work circle. Married once for five years, she admitted that her husband left because "he said I'm difficult and condescending." When one **Seasons** team member asked if she thought there was truth to his words, Jen replied, "You don't get to where I've gone by winning popularity contests." Even though Jenevieve was severely malnourished during the admission process, shaking visibly and suffering from severe withdrawal, her tone of voice reflected her ex-husband's impression.

Seasons Admission

Jenevieve had little recall of her daily life six months prior to **Seasons** admission. She had no recall of her admission into a local hospital after she called 911 that day because she feared she was dying. She remained in the hospital for several days. A battery of tests were performed to assess neurological damage done by acute alcohol poisoning over the six-month period.

During Intake, Jenevieve tended to be hostile. Her hands shook notably. Several times she stated how much she needed a drink. At one point, she became quite vocal, demanding detox medication before the session was complete. A medical staff member assured her she would be put on a comprehensive detox program. She screamed "When? I want it now!" Her son did not attempt to calm her down or offer any input during this time. The **Seasons** team decided to end the session and admit Jenevieve so she could begin the detox program.

Family History

Jenevieve described herself as a social drinker until receiving the news from her board of directors that it was "time to retire." From that point to her admission into **Seasons** six months later, her level of drinking, accompanied by severe malnourishment, had damaged her neurological system severely, enough for her family physician to initially diagnose her with Wernicke's Encephalitis. Also known as "Wet Brain" Wernicke's Encephalitis is a severe Vitamin B-1 deficiency that impacts/impairs cognitive functioning. Hearing this news from her family physician coupled with her son's profound sadness at her deteriorating condition triggered Jenevieve to seek help. Even then, she proceeded slowly. With the aid of her son, she found **Seasons in Malibu**. After intensive research and interviewing the facility and talking to several clinical staff members over many hours and days, they decided the fit was a good one. **Seasons'** one-on-one therapeutic attention, highly credentialed staff and holistic approach to treatment appealed to both Jenevieve and her son, though at Intake, she admitted to still being ambivalent about entering treatment.

Jen, as most people called her, was the third of three children born into a working class family. Her Italian immigrant father was a civil engineer in Italy but did not get credentialed in the U.S. Consequently, he worked in the steel mills in Pittsburgh during Jen's childhood, a job he loathed. To cope, he drank at night. Every night. Jenevieve described her mother as timid and fearful of her husband who tended to rage when he became intoxicated. "His message to us was always the same, 'Work hard and you can make something of yourself in this country. Don't do what I did.'" When asked to say more, Jenevieve explained that he didn't take the qualifying tests needed to become an engineer in the U.S. "I don't think he ever forgave himself for not trying."

Married only once, Jenevieve had several relationships with men but none lasting more than five years. Her ex-husband had left the marriage two years prior to her admission because she tended to berate him when she drank, though drinking was not her daily pattern back then.

Losing her job, status and access to a lifestyle she had known for so long sent Jen into a deep depression she treated daily with alcohol, from the time she woke up until she passed out. For those six months following the mandatory retirement, she lost all sense of time. She didn't eat. She didn't socialize. Jen hibernated in her condominium unless she absolutely had to leave. She had food and alcohol delivered, though she rarely ate the food. Her son had tried several times to talk her into counseling. Instead, she talked him out of his concern, mostly because he worked in another state in a career that demanded most of his time.

Jenevieve grew up watching her dad drink nightly when he came home from work. "I knew my dad depended on alcohol to get through most days. I didn't like it when I was a kid, " Jenevieve said at **Seasons** Intake meeting. She held out hands she couldn't stop from shaking. "And now look at me."

Detox

Jenevieve was placed on a detox protocol of Ativan and Phenobarbital. During this period, she remained hostile and aloof. She refused to say if **Seasons'** detox protocol helped, though staff noted less trembling and a gradual increase in her appetite. Meanwhile, the medical team reviewed the findings sent by her family physician and recommended more tests be done. While Jen was still uncooperative, her primary therapist enlisted the help of her son who, after consulting with **Seasons** medical team, agreed that more thorough testing needed to be done. Only then did Jenevieve agree to the additional medical tests.

Breaking Through! Moments In Treatment

Jenevieve was averse to twelve-step programs or any recovery groups. She did not think of herself as a "one of those" people. However, she did gravitate to **Seasons'** intensive one-on-one therapy, especially the individual work done with the recovery counselor and her individual therapist.

Individual Therapy

During the first few weeks of treatment, Jenevieve remained hostile to everyone, including her primary therapist. Often, she spoke about discharging herself against medical advice. A **Seasons** psychologist, who was her primary therapist, made the observation that "alienating" as a line of defense worked well for Jen. She consistently walled herself off from feedback delivered by other **Seasons** clients, preferring to mingle/communicate only with staff. **Seasons** clients tended to avoid her, as evidenced by Jen often dining alone. Variations of "You're doing a great job alienating yourself from other clients who could be helpful to you" were the messages consistently delivered by her primary therapist. One session in particular, Jen's therapist again referenced her condescension toward other clients, saying this: They went sideways just like you did except now they're working hard to straighten that road out in their lives. Maybe you're afraid you can't do it? This message visibly upset Jen. In the next session, Jenevieve brought up her aloofness. "I've always been this way and until now, I really didn't connect it to fear."

As trust developed, her therapist's consistent and gentle confrontation encouraged vulnerability. Eventually, Jenevieve heard this message. In time, Jen's insights included gratitude that she was able to let down her defenses/resistance to viewing the world differently. As a result, Jenevieve became her own personal scientist, hungry to know more about her "pattern of thinking" that triggered drinking. Jen's self-exploration process continued to offer insights into her life that she always described as "blessed," except historically, her life was fraught with high levels of anxiety she felt compelled to manage with alcohol. In time, Jen realized that despite her denial, she had always used alcohol as an anti-anxiety drug.

Family Therapy

Once her physical health issues were resolved, family therapy sessions offered many breakthrough moments that proved to be key in her recovery. The sessions offering significant insights into her family life came via art therapy and the use of Family Genogram,[5] a therapeutic tool rooted in family systems that offers visuals and can be helpful to many clients. Jenevieve was one of those clients. Family Genogram/timeline delivered a portrait of Jen's childhood that caused her to break down many times in sessions. This woman who adored her father began to recognize his frailties. That knowledge was difficult for Jen to absorb. She kept saying, "This makes so much sense," as new discoveries were made about her growing up years. Through the pictorial overview, Jenevieve was able to appreciate that her father came from a rigid family system and didn't find a better life than the one he left behind in Italy. He never did become the civil engineer in America that he was in his homeland. Jen was able to see how that failure influenced the way he raised his children. He was both complimentary when they succeeded and punitive when they didn't meet his expectations. A man who never lived up to his own expectations, daily drinking was the way he coped.

---

5 Family Genogram is a way of defining relationships, patterns and distinct characteristics through imagery. It allows the individual an opportunity to examine the family lineage in a different way psychologically.

Often family therapy and art therapy combined to stir up images about her growing years that had receded from Jen's recall in adult life. That is, until she was told to retire. Her reaction proved primal; if she wasn't a CEO, she wasn't anything. Jenevieve was able to appreciate that for her entire adult life, she had followed her dad's dictate to be accomplished, just as her older sister and brother had done.

Transformative sessions included her son's role in their family system. She began to realize that while she adored him, she had always been very hard on him, much as her father had been on her. "It was always for his benefit because I knew he was so smart," Jenevieve said during a session about parent expectations. Fortunately, her son was able to take a leave from his hospital duties to attend several family sessions. He was willing to talk about his obsessive-compulsive disorder, which, as he grew older, he was finding harder to manage. Jenevieve was able to trace much of its beginnings to very stressful times in his young life.

Often during family therapy, Jenevieve remarked how fortunate she was to receive these gifts of understanding about her family and herself. "My dad must have loathed himself for failing to be what he thought he should have been. How could he pass on anything but that to his kids?"

Meeting TREATMENT Goals

It became clear within days of admission that Jen was too depressed and physically compromised to be an active participant in her care. Detox was difficult and staff were concerned that organic factors, such as her brain functioning, could influence her ability to engage. Subsequent to the request for additional testing, the medical team delivered good news. Jen had not permanently damaged her neurological system and once stable, she was expected to make a full mental recovery. That day proved to be the turning point in Jen's participation in treatment. At the end of her sixty-day agreed upon stay, she requested an extension. "I'm just beginning to figure me out. I can't stop now," she said to her primary therapist. She meant it.

At Discharge

Discharged after ninety days, Jen's aftercare program included individual therapy sessions twice weekly with a **Seasons**-recommended psychologist, ongoing recovery work with a sober coach and a commitment to find and integrate into healthy social groups.

During treatment, Jenevieve expressed interest in helping young people, especially girls. A nationwide non-profit had asked her to join the board soon after she left her company. She liked the organization very much but ignored the invitation. Two days before discharge, she reconnected with the group and accepted. They were thrilled. "I think I now have something to say to young girls," she offered to her primary therapist. When asked to elaborate, Jenevieve replied, "Make sure you're kind to yourself. No matter what you accomplish, make sure you take care of yourself first."

WHATEVER I NEED TO DO!
Austin, Texas: Episodic Alcoholic Drinking/Anger Management

Matt, a forty-one-year-old attorney living in Austin Texas, was an episodic drinker who often raged when he became inebriated. In all likelihood, a collision of cultures factored into Matt's violent outburst on the night he aimed his handgun at his wife and demanded she listen to him. Fortunately, she was able to remove herself and their young son from harm's way. Once outside their home, she called the police. They arrived and arrested Matt who kept repeating that the gun was not loaded. At **Seasons** Intake, he said again that he would never hurt his wife. What he wanted her to do was listen to him.

At the interview, a team member asked about his wife's response on the night of his arrest. Matt shifted his gaze to the floor. When he looked up, his voice was barely audible. "She said to me, 'You pointed that gun at my head, the mother of your little boy, you pointed that gun at my head.' She kept saying that…" Matt looked away again. After a short pause he spoke, his voice much stronger. "Whatever I need to do, I'll do it. Whatever it is. I have to fix this."

Meet Matt:
Austin Texas
Episodic Alcoholic Drinking/Anger Management

Matt was a forty-one-year-old attorney from Austin, Texas who came from a wealthy family. Throughout the **Seasons** Intake, embarrassment and shame emanated from this attorney whose family name was recognized in Texas. His eyes remained fixed on the floor and he spoke softly. Matt admitted himself to **Seasons in Malibu**. Due to the restraining order on him when he entered treatment, Matt's wife could not be present at Intake. Though willing to participate in her husband's treatment, a formal legal filing had to be cleared before she could join him in meetings.

Occasionally throughout the Intake interview, Matt wiped his eyes with the handkerchief he held. A domestic violence arrest brought him to **Seasons in Malibu**. Matt was an episodic drinker and when he did indulge, he tended to lose control of his temper, behavior his wife, a 39-year-old woman of Latino descent, had not witnessed when her husband was sober. Never had he come close to doing what he did the night she called the police after successfully removing herself and their little boy from their residence in Austin. Moments before she safely made their exit, Matt waved a handgun at her, one of several from his gun collection, and demanded that she shut up and listen to him. She did so immediately as she also began ushering their seven-year-old boy toward the kitchen door.

As she exited the house, Matt repeated, "It's not loaded! It's not loaded! I just want you to listen to me!" over and over but by then, her only concern was for the safety of their child.

Seasons Admission

By the time he admitted himself, Matt had a fairly clear understanding of the dynamics in his family that had led him to rage-filled outbursts. Due to the court order, it took one week to gain permission for Matt's wife Lisa to join him in therapy sessions. Though she could not attend the Intake session, they did communicate by phone during the session.

Seasons in Malibu's well-known treatment modalities in trauma and cognitive behavioral therapies aid in understanding how past experiences impact the present, often without a client's knowledge. Matt related to this perspective, as did his wife. Though they were still living apart, she was willing to give him a second chance and planned to temporarily move to the area with their son so she could participate in family and couples therapy sessions. He expressed his gratitude several times during Intake stating that without her support, he would be on much less solid ground.

Family History

Matt and Lisa had been married for ten years and both were working full-time when he voluntarily entered treatment at **Seasons in Malibu**. Matt's wife was an executive in the marketing industry. They had one child, a seven-year-old son. Matt described his childhood as traditionally Southern; his father was the head of the household and his mother subservient to him. Matt was more academic than athletic and the first of three children to earn a degree from an Ivy League school. His father was in manufacturing and his mother, a housewife, passed away five years earlier and two years after Matt's son was born. Matt described his relationship to a younger sister and brother as close; both lived about one hour from his home. He did not mention his father until a **Seasons** team member asked about him. He was still alive, quite elderly, a man Matt described as "punitive as ever."

Matt had not been in any therapeutic environment until his arrest. Part of his parole included mandatory anger management group sessions. In one of these sessions, Matt acknowledged that the severe punishments his father inflicted on his children were abusive. "His belt and a switch was how he disciplined us." When asked to say more, Matt added, "That's the way it was so I didn't think of it as abuse back then. Not until I had my son did I even realize how harsh my father was." Still, Matt did not label his dad's punishments as abuse until he discovered in anger management sessions that every group member had experienced some sort of abuse when they were youngsters. "That's when I knew he was abusive. No child should be hit by his parent like that."

Matt described himself as quiet, even passive, most of the time, much like his mother. He described his wife as "very loud." As the eldest daughter of a large Latino family, Lisa took on the role of family caretaker. She multitasked quite well but often by ignoring input from others, including her husband, a personality trait she recognized as problematic. The incident that resulted in his arrest centered on Matt's request being ignored again. He specifically had told Lisa he did not want to attend a family party she insisted they attend. On the evening of the party and after downing several shots of whiskey, Matt said he just "went off." He also said it wasn't the first time. His pattern of drinking included binge episodes every five to six months. He would get intoxicated enough to trigger his temper, which was always accompanied by really intense feelings. "I sweep everything under the carpet until I have a few and then ..." The night of this incident, he took a revolver from a locked cabinet where he kept his gun collection, aimed it at Lisa, and demanded she listen to his rant about not being heard. She was able to lead their son out of the house, and once removed, she called the police. They arrested Matt that night. Since his arrest, he had followed every provision of his parole including the sixteen anger management sessions he had completed before his **Seasons** admission. These sessions triggered Matt's desire to get help with core issues driving his behavior; issues rooted in his childhood. He wanted to understand more about how his past had influenced his behavior. This is why he decided to enter treatment at **Seasons in Malibu**.

Detox

When Matt entered **Seasons**, he did not need detoxification. His drinking was episodic and he hadn't had a drink since the night of his arrest twenty weeks earlier.

Community Based Support Groups

During the first two weeks, Matt eagerly attended all recovery-related meetings. He gravitated toward the message in SMART Recovery, particularly those messages that utilize evidence-based interventions and strategies about sobriety. Matt related to how an individual's behavior and thinking can impact understanding of sobriety.

Breaking Through! Moments In Treatment

Individual Therapy

Growing up with mixed messages was often the focus in Matt's individual therapy sessions. He so detested how his father raised him that as an adult, he wanted no part of carrying out his traditions. Yet when his wife did not defer to him, he often seethed. In time, he recognized that he was acting out a scenario from childhood. At a conscious level, Matt was drawn to women unlike his mother which was why Lisa was so attractive to him when they met. Back then he wanted no part of recreating his upbringing. Yet, at some level, he did. "Sometimes, I'd get so mad when she'd disagree with me and often it'd be over stupid stuff," he said. No one ever disagreed with his father and the lingering effect of that was often the focus of his individual sessions.

Family/Couples Therapy

Matt and Lisa attended couples and family therapy sessions from the second week through discharge, five weeks later. Matt's family history and his expectations remained a major focus for many sessions. Both agreed that during their courtship, engaging in these kinds of conversations would have been helpful in understanding one another. "Opposites attract" explained their initial attraction. She was verbal, he wasn't. She came from a large Latino family where everybody had an opinion they tended to share loudly. Like most firstborns in traditional families where gender roles were entrenched, Matt had expectations to perform at a certain level, which he did by becoming the first one to earn entrance into an Ivy League university. His wife's family background was similar. Lisa was the first girl to earn an advanced degree and continue working even after her son was born. Her senior level position included managing a team of marketing reps. After Lisa had some time to express her fear and reservations about moving forward in their marriage, she did begin to appreciate how each of them had to shift some life long behaviors if they expected a different result.

Two weeks before discharge, Matt and Lisa's only child was brought into family sessions to explore his recollection of that night. These sessions were heart-felt and their son seemed relieved to be able to share and ask questions about that night. "Are you getting divorced?" he asked several times during the first session. Both of them assured him that they would do everything they could to remain a family.

Group Therapy

In SMART Recovery meetings, Matt talked about being a Southern man, the eldest in a family that included expectations to perform well at all times. As a young man, he struggled to confront his father but never did.

The expectations of compliance, unspoken in his family, left Matt feeling discouraged and unsupported throughout most of his life. In one session, Matt connected "those dots" to the unspoken expectations he had of his wife—to comply with his wishes just as his mother had complied with his father's—an insight that Matt appreciated learning. "I never said it but I did expect her to comply even though I knew I was marrying a strong-willed woman. That was a huge attraction for me. Lisa was not afraid to speak her mind." From that point on, and with the aid of work he had been doing in anger management classes, Matt kept his focus on recognizing triggers for his anger and learning ways to discharge it constructively.

Supportive/Complementary Therapies

IMAGO, a therapeutic technique used in couples therapy, was utilized with success. Latin for "image" IMAGO specifically works with couples by role-playing how to effectively listen and validate, rather than be defensive and argumentative. The emphasis is on allowing one to have a voice and to be heard. Being heard doesn't always mean being "agreed with," an insight that both Matt and Lisa appreciated learning.

Meeting TREATMENT Goals

From the first day of admission, SMART Recovery meetings, couples therapy (including IMAGO sessions) and family therapy made a significant impact on Matt. He often repeated how knowledge is power and that he should have figured this out sooner. "Maybe my wife wouldn't have to live with that memory," he said at one SMART Recovery session and then broke down and sobbed. Group members were quite supportive. Based on the interactions staff observed, Matt was able to accept their kindness, another first for Matt, who grew up believing that men did not show emotions because it was a sign of weakness.

At Discharge

Matt, scheduled for discharge after a six-week stay, extended his stay by two weeks. During that time, he and the **Seasons** team planned for his discharge and return to Austin. Matt wanted to replicate the treatment delivered at **Seasons** so he found a SMART Recovery group and began attending the Austin chapter's online meetings while still at **Seasons**. The anger management classes he attended in Austin offered advanced groups focused on learning. To maintain his law license, Matt had to attend additional anger management groups, so he signed up for Saturday morning sessions. The couple continued with a therapist trained in the IMAGO style of couple's therapy. The role modeling visual really worked for Matt and Lisa. Their work together remained centered on acquiring healthy, productive ways of handling family/couples conflicts. The court eventually granted Matt the opportunity to return home and restraining orders were terminated.

He was placed on supervised probation for three years with monthly progress reports sent to his law license oversight committee.

Matt returned to his law practice, and eighteen months later, he and Lisa welcomed a second child into their family.

I FOUND THE RIGHT PLACE
Los Angeles/Salt Lake City, Utah: Meth/Poly-Drug Abuse

"I was a pretty smart kid," Steven offered at the **Seasons** Intake interview. "I've known since I was six or seven that I was different. By nine, I knew what that difference was. I much preferred boys to girls."

Steven, raised in Salt Lake City, Utah, came from a devout Mormon family. He was a thirty-nine year old medical doctor recently relieved from his duties at an urgent care facility. Two weeks prior to his **Seasons** admission, he walked the streets of West Hollywood looking for his next high. He had not slept in days and couldn't remember the last meal he had consumed. His only concern was getting that next snort of meth, by then his drug of choice. On the day he hit bottom, Steven was walking down Santa Monica Boulevard looking to score more meth and happened upon a store window. His reflection in the window so unnerved him he couldn't return to work. Several days later, he was called in by the professional Wellness Committee and put on suspension. When this happened, he called a friend who had recently conquered his own *demons and was living a sober life. His friend came over and once he saw Steven, immediately contacted his family. Steven needed an intervention.*

Though his father and several siblings traveled from Utah and other states to attend the meeting, Steven's mother refused to attend. The fact that Steven was at risk of dying due to his drug addiction was secondary to her concern about her son's sexuality. Steven came out to his parents when he graduated from medical school. Since then, he had very little contact with any family members, including an older sister who had left the family many years earlier once she turned eighteen.

Meet Steven:
Los Angeles/Salt Lake City, Utah
Meth/Poly-Drug Abuse

Steven, a 39-year-old medical doctor, continuously picked at his nail beds and wiped his nose during the **Seasons** Intake interview. He hadn't taken his drug of choice, Methamphetamine, for six days but had been self-medicating with anti-anxiety drugs and alcohol to reduce his withdrawal symptoms. Though in obvious physical distress, he kept assuring the treatment team that his fidgetiness did not reflect ambivalence. "I need to be here. I found the right place. This has got to end or I will. It's that simple."

Steven attributed his dependence on drugs to anxiety he felt from a very young age, anxiety caused from knowing he was different from the other children in his Mormon community. One of eight children born to a middle-class Mormon couple, Steven understood his addiction as a consequence of being the gay son of very religious and influential Mormon parents. "You have no idea how much I've shamed my parents," he repeated several times during his initial interview. Reinforcing his point, he added, "My mother really can't be around me. Any concern she has is not about my addiction. It's about my sexuality. She cannot abide by it and it's caused her great pain and embarrassment in our community."

After returning from a two-year mission, a rite of passage Mormon boys go through before attending college, Steven applied to and was accepted at several California universities. Once home from his mission, his mother began matchmaking; a stream of Mormon girls was invited for Sunday dinners. Steven knew the only way to avoid the scene was to leave. He moved to California, where he earned his undergraduate degree and attended medical school.

Steven had his first homosexual relationship at age twenty-eight, the year he graduated from medical school. His poly-drug abuse also began at this time, introduced by his lover, a man who told him cocaine enhanced the sexual experience. Steven claimed he used it only "recreationally" until his lover left him two years later. His descent into addiction took a serious dive when he was introduced to meth, described to him as "the cheap cousin of cocaine." He needed the stimulant to put in the twelve- to eighteen-hour days at the medical walk-in clinic where he worked. Cocaine was too expensive. "I was told it was the same high except it wasn't. From my first hit, I was totally hooked," he said.

Within two years of habitual meth use, the clinic where Steven worked had reported him to their overseeing health and wellness board due to his many absences and multiple errors. He was placed on leave and given a list of Professional Treatment Programs approved by the medical board. He chose **Seasons in Malibu** Treatment Center's Professionals Treatment Program, highly regarded in the field and strict in its adherence to guidelines set by the California overseeing medical board.

Seasons Admission

Steven was admitted via the Professionals Treatment Program offered by **Seasons in Malibu** for professionals struggling with addictions. The comprehensive program

includes a Clinical Diagnostic Evaluation (CDE) administered over three days. The results recommended that
Steven could benefit the most from ninety days of residential treatment to address issues related to his substance
use and situational depression.

Steven was admitted to **Seasons** accompanied by his
father and sister. Though Steven had asked both parents
to attend family therapy sessions, his mother refused. His
father did agree to attend though initially his only concern centered on his son's sexuality. He wanted to know
how Steven could fix his sexuality so that he could "raise
a family" like most of his siblings were doing. Steven mentioned his older sister who had left Utah at age eighteen
and never returned. He was ten when she left home and
added that she had not maintained contact with any family member. A team member asked Steven's father about
this daughter. He replied that he didn't know anything
more than what Steven had offered. She just left. Then
a team member asked if he understood the seriousness of
his son's addiction. His reply indicated that the root of
Steven's addiction was his sexuality. "I think that's why he
uses drugs," his father said.

Family History

Steven's father was a church elder and his mother managed one of the church affiliated nursery schools in Salt
Lake City. As a child, Steven excelled in school and was
given much encouragement by his parents to become a

medical doctor. Though he was always an obedient child, from a young age, he knew something was different. He described feeling anxious throughout most of his childhood, an anxiety he dealt with by being obsessive-compulsive about his study habits and his cleanliness. As he grew into adolescence, he recognized that difference for what it was; he was attracted to the boys in his school, not the girls.

Though Steven was thirty-nine years old when he was admitted to **Seasons**, his understanding of gender roles and sexuality seemed dated. One staff member described it as "adolescent." He had not sought out support groups for gay people raised in religious homes nor had he disconnected from the Mormon Church. He did not attend services but listed "Mormon" as his religion. Much of his dialogue during early interactions at **Seasons** revolved around shame and sin.

Detox

For six days before admission, Steven had not used Meth. To manage his withdrawal, he drank vodka and took Valium. Once admitted, he was placed on a detox protocol and for the first four days, he was visibly uncomfortable, though his discomfort did not keep him from participating in the program or any activity.

Community Based Support Groups

Steven was somewhat familiar with the Alcoholics Anonymous twelve–step program and though he had attended a few meetings in the past, he did not connect. At one A.A. meeting, a member asked if Steven knew about the twelve-step LGBT meetings. Steven was shocked to know that they existed. **Seasons** staff arranged for him to attend those meetings as well as the "Professionals Caduceus Meetings for Medical Professionals." From his first meetings with both twelve-step support groups, Steven felt "at home" and described both groups as "good fits."

Breaking Through! Moments In Treatment

Individual Therapy

A **Seasons** clinical psychologist was specifically asked to be at Steven's Intake interview because in addition to her clinical expertise, she often worked with clients whose crises include sexuality and religion as central issues. At the end of the Intake interview, she asked Steven if he wanted to work individually with her. It was the only time he managed a smile during that lengthy session. "Thank you. I was going to ask you."

Initially, feelings of shame were the focus of individual therapy. The shame that he brought to his family, his mother in particular, he could easily discuss in sessions. But when she asked about his shame, Steven did not make connections as easily. At one session, his primary therapist was quite specific: Let's talk about the shame of throwing your good life away just because you don't fit your parents' idea of what a spiritual person should look like. It took Steven some time to reply. When he did, he led with, "That's a damn good point you just made."

Steven was also able to work with a renowned spiritual therapist **Seasons** has on staff who helped facilitate his understanding of his own spiritual path. The focus of Steven's spiritual work centered on helping him define his own religious/spiritual belief system that he could find comfort in. Eventually, this helped him find distance from his parents' punitive messages that centered on religion. Steven's need to find a new path to his spiritual higher self was discovered in these sessions. Those insights paved the way for his shift in thinking that ultimately led to a change in his behavior.

Being raised in a very religious home—the good, the bad and the ugly—was easily understood by both his primary therapist and spiritual therapist. Steven struggled to find his identity outside of his religious upbringing. At admission, all he saw was his failure. From the start, Steven worked hard to uncover the layers of his own self-loathing. He could not do anything about anyone else's opinion of him but he could become strong enough to be all that he could be without the need to be self-destructive. He could learn to love himself that much. This became his overall treatment goal. "I should have been dead but I'm not. Maybe that's my God speaking to me."

Family Therapy

The value of family therapy sessions that include family members who may not be supportive is to give clients the opportunity to be a witness to behaviors that need to be "seen to be understood." Of all the interventions and therapies Steven embraced, family systems intrigued him the most. He devoured several books in the **Seasons'** library and asked for ongoing recommendations. Steven was especially drawn to literature that offered stories about people raised in devout religious homes finding spiritual nourishment elsewhere. He appreciated information regarding the significance of birth order and the role "identified patients" play in family dysfunction. Identified patients are typically labeled as the "sick one" in a family system. He absorbed this information as if he were a student of the subject. At first, Steven wondered how he had managed to avoid psychology classes about family dynamics during his undergraduate and medical school education. Before long, Steven began to understand his lack of knowledge as he linked it to his upbringing: His self-loathing was linked to the self he was taught to love but could never be: a heterosexual male. In one session, Steven said, "When you drink the Kool-Aid, no matter how smart you are, that's your perspective."

Group Therapy

In one LGBT A.A. meeting, Steven shared that for the first time, he felt like he was gaining control over his life that had been out of control for the last seven years. Peer support among LGBT members felt like "family" to Steven.

The professional meetings he was required to attend gave him a platform to work through his shame about using drugs while practicing medicine. **Seasons** also helped Steven connect to a group of LGBT Ex-Mormons who embraced a spiritual path and faith that was inclusive rather than exclusive.

Supportive and Complementary Treatments

Steven embraced holistic treatments offered at **Seasons** that included yoga, cranial-sacral massage and meditation. He loved yoga because the practice connected him to his body that he had tried so hard to destroy. Often he became teary-eyed at the end of a session, one of the few times Steven showed emotion. After one evening practice, he rested in Shevasana (this pose ends a practice and often triggers emotions), Steven began to cry. "Tears of joy," he said when invited to share. He had had an epiphany. His reckless behavior did not leave him dead or infected. At this post yoga "informal" session, Steven decided to view his life as a miracle and proceed accordingly.

Meeting Treatment Goals

Steven was grateful to his dad who traveled twice during his ninety-day **Seasons** stay to attend family therapy sessions. At Steven's request, his dad also attended a few sessions with his primary therapist. The three met twice: one session midway through treatment and one session during discharge week.

During the last session, Steven turned toward his father and said, "In the absence of my parents and church, I think what I was doing was carrying out my own punishment." His dad sat silent but as Steven began to speak again, he managed to look over at his son. Steven thanked his father for supporting him through treatment, acknowledging that he knew it was difficult. "You're not like me and I'm not like you," Steven said. His father nodded in agreement. The contrast of what he had managed to accomplish despite his self-loathing behaviors continued to be explored in all therapeutic interactions. By the time Steven left, he said it all made sense.

At Discharge

Professionals Program Requirements: When he entered treatment, Steven's troubles with the professional wellness committee were unresolved. **Seasons'** Professionals Program helped him prioritize steps that needed to be taken prior to discharge. **Seasons** maintained a rigorous schedule of communication with his wellness committee and identified specific recommendations post-treatment. Some of these recommendations included ongoing participation in twelve-step programs, sponsorship, random drug screening, ongoing therapy, ongoing participation in the professionals group and monitoring by the recommended monitoring board. He was grateful to have the opportunity to salvage his career but also for the level of insight and improved understanding he had regarding his drug abuse and his sexuality.

Steven met with his wellness committee immediately upon discharge. With the full discharge report completed by the **Seasons** staff, the wellness committee decided that Steven would follow the recommendations and allowed him to return to work part-time with a strategy to full-time as long as he continued to remain compliant.

He continued individual therapy sessions with his **Seasons** primary therapist. The team helped Steven find an Ex-Mormon sponsor, and prior to discharge, Steven joined an LGBT twelve-step program near his apartment. He also remained in his professionals group. Before discharge, his case manager helped him find a "recovering" Mormon support group online. Steven was shocked to discover members who were transparently gay. For the first time in his life, Steven felt real hope for the future.

Post Discharge Update

Since he was working part-time, Steven volunteered at an L.A. LGBT Center that included a teen crisis hotline.

He was asked if he would be open to discussing the link between sexuality, religion and drugs on the L.A. LGBT center podcast. Within minutes of the podcast airing, the hotline lit up with calls from gay kids from UBER religious homes. Steven had found his calling. He decided to spend much of his time administering to the hotline program. Eventually, he took it over and expanded it to include interviews with experts working with the LGBT population in the clinical, academic and religious sectors. His **Seasons** primary therapist was among his first interviews and she became a show consultant.

THE GAMBLER AND FAMILY SECRETS
Seattle/Las Vegas: Opiate, Sexual and Poly-drug Abuse

Sean, a thirty-three-year-old professional poker player from Seattle, Washington, made millions of dollars in Las Vegas before turning thirty. He became quite well known, especially after starring on the highest rated poker game show on cable TV. It was on that show that he hit "bottom" publicly by falling asleep at the table after placing a half million-dollar bet. Recalling that day, he said, "I should have snorted a line of coke but I forgot how much Vic I'd taken until I was at that table. Then it was too late."

His head smacked the table hard enough to cause the audience to gasp loudly before the show cut to a commercial and Sean was carried off the stage. He was snoring. As a result of that incident, the five hundred thousand dollar loss at the table was only one of many he endured. The show cancelled his appearances and once the news spread, he not only lost credibility but also all the perks of being one of the youngest and most successful poker players Las Vegas had ever known.

"I actually don't remember the last few months including that night," Sean said to the **Seasons** Intake team. Though the cable station was able to edit out most of that scene, word spread fast in this city where he was well known. Though his recall of the previous six months was limited, Sean assumed that his fall from grace increased his drug usage. To earn money for Vicodin and other drugs and also pay bills that included a mortgage, he disguised himself as a tourist and entered pick-up poker games. At Intake he said he easily won enough to keep this lifestyle going.

Sean's decision to get help happened after an incident occurred one week prior to his **Seasons** admission. He was a no-show at a game his poker-playing friend needed him to be at, so the friend went to Sean's condo and found him on the floor unconscious. His breathing, shallow and uneven, alarmed his friend enough to call 911. Though Sean was released from the hospital the next day, the E.R. doctor told him the next time he probably would not be so lucky. *"He said I was literally a few minutes away from death."*

Sean came to **Seasons** without family or friends and described himself as a loner, even when he was a child. *"I don't come from the kind of family you'd want around anyway."*

Meet Sean:
Seattle/Las Vegas
Opiate, Sexual and Poly-drug Abuse

Sean is a thirty-three-year-old professional gambler with a prescription drug addiction—his drug of choice: Vicodin. Sean came to **Seasons** after overdosing on Vicodin and almost dying. He became addicted soon after a weight lifting incident left him in chronic back pain. His doctor initially prescribed Vicodin until Sean showed signs of dependence. Though his doctor switched him to non-opiate pain relievers, Sean was easily able to get his drug of choice from other physicians.

Sean, an enormously successful young man, spent his twenties being the "darling" of the Las Vegas strip. A child prodigy, his mathematical aptitude was channeled into gambling at a very young age. He made his first million dollars by age twenty-two. He had very little to do with his family, which included a father, older sister and younger brother. His mother died of ovarian cancer five years prior to Sean's admission. Of interest, soon after his mom died, he suffered a severe back injury lifting weights—the injury that began his Vicodin dependence. Also in the past five years, Sean had lived with seven different women.

Until the last few years, he was able to keep gambling for a living and gambling for his own pleasure separate. However, as his addiction became unmanageable, he accrued a gambling debt of one million dollars that his lenders expected him to pay off.

Seasons Admission

Sean came to **Seasons** alone. He had no family in Vegas and described his family in Seattle as "crazy." When asked for more information, Sean reported that he was raised in a three-room slum dwelling in the outskirts of Seattle. His sister only made contact when she needed money and he hadn't seen a younger brother in fifteen years. His mother had passed and his father, a heavy drinker, was a retired auto mechanic. Sean had not seen him since he left home the day after graduating from high school. He stated emphatically that he did not want to ever see him again.

Family History

Sean described his childhood as sad. He said he saw things kids shouldn't see but during Intake, he did not offer more details. Later, in his first individual therapy session, Sean said this about his father's participation in treatment: He is dead to me. What he did to my sister and brother should not be forgiven.

Due to his unhappy home environment, Sean spent much time on the streets in a neighborhood where drive-by shootings were not unusual. It felt safer than home. Sean had no awareness of his natural aptitude for mathematical patterns and memorization until he landed his first job at age twelve, running numbers for several gamblers. They told him how unusual his talents were and in no time, they taught him how to play poker. Soon after that, Sean was sponsored by name brands to play poker in arenas that didn't allow minors, though they always made an exception for him. By the time he turned eighteen, he was on his way to becoming a top-ranked poker player. He left Seattle for Las Vegas, and within a few years, he became a well-known gambling professional there. Soon poker players from around the world were traveling to Las Vegas to play at his table. With that kind of attention came many women that Sean did not turn away. Once settled into treatment, Sean began to identify himself as addicted to sex as well as drugs and gambling. He told his primary therapist that he would often mix cocaine with Viagra and enjoy the company of several women in one night. However, despite the attention, he continued to feel lonely.

His sister participated in several tele-sessions but Sean's younger brother could not be found. At age eighteen, he too left home, but for a life on the streets. Several years ago, Sean found out he was somewhere in Asia making adult films for a living. Sean said that of the three, his younger brother was the most damaged. Once Sean and his sister moved away, he was left alone to deal with the madness that took place in that apartment.

During the first few weeks, Sean did not talk much about his family but when he did, his father was usually the topic. Each time his mother was mentioned, he would offer short answers that always centered on her physical weakness due to her diminutive size and his father's violent behavior toward her when he was drunk.

Detox

Sean was placed on a Suboxone taper that weaned him slowly from opiates. For the first several days, detox was difficult; he was agitated and non-communicative in all groups. At mealtime, he chose to seclude himself and when people did sit at his table, he would quickly finish his meal and leave. As his physical discomfort decreased, he began to participate in treatment more readily.

Community Based Support Groups

Sean engaged in the SMART Recovery sessions and found them very applicable to his life, particularly since he was a "numbers" guy and tended to relate to straightforward and logical kind of thinking. He also embraced the Sex and Love Anonymous (SLA) groups, which provided a safe and non-judgmental haven for him to share his sexual compulsions, which he also dealt with in his individual therapy sessions.

Breaking Through! Moments In Treatment

Individual Therapy

Initially, individual sessions with his psychologist focused on his early childhood and family, though he did not talk about his mother unless specifically asked. In time, Sean began to bring her up in sessions. He wondered if she was sexually abused, too. "She never fought for herself or for us...I would get so mad but it was like she had no strength to fight...so she just said nothing about all those late-night visits." By the time he moved out, Sean hated both parents and lost all contact until a month before his mother's death from untreated ovarian cancer. His sister informed him. "I would have given her money for treatment," he said. For several sessions, he talked of life regrets, specifically as they related to his mother. "None of us, we never talked," he said of his family's pattern of behavior. As therapy sessions progressed, Sean's attitude about his parents began to shift from indicting to wondering what had happened to them, his mother especially, during their childhoods that caused them both to be so damaged. He knew that both parents lived in abject poverty for their entire childhoods. "The only grandparent I ever met was illiterate. I remember my mother describing her family as 'trailer trash.' Maybe compared to them, we had it easy. At least we had an apartment and both of my parents could read."

Sean had no notion of psychology, including addiction treatment, when he entered **Seasons**. During his stay, he became fascinated by family systems, compulsive disorders and addiction principles he learned. Sean began to appreciate that his childhood was focused solely on surviving and therefore he had no idea how to communicate at a personal level. He never learned how. His image of himself was formed early and centered on his outstanding accomplishments, not his feelings. He said often in sessions that he couldn't imagine a woman falling in love with him if he had nothing to offer but himself. "Why would she want me?" he often asked.

Family Therapy

Sean's sister could not attend family therapy except for a few telephone sessions. Though she tried to support Sean, she stated emphatically that she did not want to talk about her past. Sean had no other family or significant others to attend sessions so most of his exposure/understanding of family dynamics came through group sessions, which educated and enlightened him regarding the value of boundaries and family systems. Sean enjoyed listening during these group discussions and tended to bring topics into his individual sessions. Sean requested more information about family systems and how destructive behaviors, without intervention or awareness, just get passed on through the generations. **Seasons'** library offered a substantial supply of family theory/therapy oriented books that Sean enjoyed reading. In time, he realized that though he lived in close proximity to a lot of people during his childhood, he had no sense of living in a functional family system.

In S.L.A. meetings and elsewhere, Sean began to connect his impulsivity toward women with his generalized impulsivity. "It's one reason why I'm in this mess. The minute money hits my hands, I give it away. With women? I fall in love immediately." Many members understood this behavior, which surprised Sean. "I thought I was the only one," he often said during and after these self-help sessions.

Supportive and Complementary Treatments

During his early years in Las Vegas, Sean befriended a hypnotist who worked in clubs on the Strip. Sean had been hypnotized and trusted this process. He believed hypnosis had helped him gain confidence at the poker table, so he was open to working with the **Seasons** hypnotherapist. Not familiar with "therapeutic" hypnosis, he was curious and agreed to a few sessions to see "what would come up." He hoped it would help ease torturous memories of witnessing incest countless nights when his father came into the bedroom that Sean shared with his siblings. The weekly sessions proved helpful. It did help ease memories. It also helped him envision himself as something other than a gambler.

Meeting TREATMENT Goals

Sean wanted to shift from professional gambler to a profession that incorporated his overall aptitude, especially his mathematical capabilities. **Seasons** staff suggested that he might benefit from a psychological assessment, which would offer a realistic snapshot of his overall capacity to learn and thrive in other areas. Additionally, Sean began to understand that his fear of intimacy at any level was directly connected to early childhood trauma. In Sex and Love Anonymous, Sean learned that oftentimes, molested children grow up to be addicted to sexual attention because they associate it with caring. After particularly rough therapy sessions, he often said he felt better because he understood more.

At Discharge

Sean was discharged after sixty days of treatment, with a solid ninety-day outpatient plan in place. An S.L.A. sponsor was secured in Las Vegas as well as a psychologist who was also a certified hypnotherapist. Sean's goal, to apply his considerable math skills to a new line of work, began to take form during his **Seasons** stay. Thanks to the psychological testing, he recognized that he was more than qualified to participate in a number of professional fields. One of those he desired was finance. He applied to a community college to begin his bachelor's degree in mathematics and started taking core classes on-line while still in treatment at **Seasons in Malibu**.

Post-Discharge Update

Once he returned to Las Vegas, Sean quickly recognized that remaining there would be difficult. On two separate occasions, he relapsed and knew that he could not continue to live in that city. He also was not following through with the recommended aftercare plan. Fortunately, he reached out to his **Seasons** Case Manager for support. They came up with a plan.

Sean sold his lavish condo in Las Vegas and relocated to Los Angeles. He entered into a **Seasons**-recommended outpatient program and found a local S.L.A. group. Additionally, he began community college and started working part-time as a financial analyst for a mortgage company located in downtown L.A. Sean continued his college courses and met a woman during this time.

Five years post-**Seasons** discharge, Sean had reconciled his gambling debts, married and moved to Santa Barbara, California. He and his wife have a two-year-old daughter. He works as a wealth manager for a major brokerage firm and he is sober.

About the Authors

Mark Stahlhuth, Ph.D., was born in Michigan, raised in Colorado and after moving to Southern California, attended U.C.L.A. He entered California School of Professional Psychology, Alliant University, to complete his doctorate in clinical psychology, which included extensive training in psycho-diagnostic assessment. In addition to conducting psychological assessments for over three decades, Dr. Stahlhuth has worked in the addiction field since 1980. For twenty-seven years, he worked in the adult and adolescent residential field treating addiction, sexual abuse and trauma. In 1995, he opened a private practice specializing in the treatment of families suffering from addiction and trauma. In 2009, Dr Stahlhuth became Clinical Director for **Seasons Recovery Centers**

in Malibu. He utilizes his extensive experience in addiction treatment and trauma resolution to orchestrate the cutting edge clinical programs that **Seasons** is known for; programs that include a residential trauma tract for clients whose primary issue underlying self-medicating addiction is past trauma. This tract was developed by Dr. Stahlhuth.

In 1985, **Dr. Nancy Irwin** moved to New York City from her hometown Atlanta to pursue a career in stand-up comedy. She enjoyed success performing around the country and abroad, until a volunteering experience in a Los Angeles shelter housing sexually abused teenagers proved life-changing, enough to shift her career goals from entertainment to psychology. Soon after, she enrolled in California Southern University, earning a doctorate in psychology with a focus on prevention and healing of sexual abuse. After earning her credentials, as well as a certification in hypnotherapy, Dr. Irwin became a frequent guest on many radio and television talk shows including CNN, FOX, CNBC, MSNBC.

Of her many awards and accolades, Dr Irwin holds memberships in the California Psychological Association, the Association for Treatment of Sexual Abusers,

Diplomate in the American Academy of Experts in Traumatic Stress and the American Hypnosis Association.

A powerful keynote speaker, Dr. Irwin's message is: Change does not have to be scary and hard. It can be creative and fun.

Full biographies of all Seasons in Malibu clinicians, including books and publications, on www.seasonsmalibu.com

ACKNOWLEDGMENTS

Seasons In Malibu Addiction Treatment Center is grateful to all of our clients, former, present and future, for trusting us with their health. It is because of them that we decided to write *Breaking Through! Stories of Hope and Recovery.*

Our gratitude also extends to **Seasons Recovery Centers'** Chief Operating Officer, Dr. Sheila Shilati, for planting the seed that grew into this collection of stories. Her input throughout this process was beyond significant. Our thanks to **Seasons In Malibu's** C.E.O./Founder, Don Varden, who envisioned a book filled with intimate stories that also delivered critical information about treatment. Our sincere thanks to Marla Miller, developmental editor and psychiatric nurse practitioner, for her help in crafting the stories told in *Breaking Through! Stories of Hope and Recovery.* To Susan Segal/editor/USC professor and novelist, our sincere thanks for polishing this manuscript. To David Wogahn of AuthorImprints.com, thank you for the beautifully designed print and ebook showcasing

Seasons in Malibu stories of hope. We also want to thank Matt Ramage of Emarketed for his cover art and design.

Dr. Mark Stahlhuth and Dr. Nancy Irwin

**Contact Seasons In Malibu
World Class Addiction Treatment via
website, www.SeasonsMalibu.com
and/or call 866-780-8539.**